SIMON
OF
CYRENE

Nabil ZIANI

Ordering Information:

Prime Seven Media
518 Landmann St.
Tomah City, WI 54660

Printed in the United States of America

Table of Contents

FOREWORD

The history of Christianity begins, in most of the books devoted to it, in the second century, as literature and documents become available which tell the story and attest to it. Concerning the first century, most of the accounts revolve around the character of the Apostle Paul, a first-rate evangelist, who tirelessly proclaimed the Gospel in Asia Minor and in Europe, until his death as a martyr in Rome in the sixties. In most contemporary Bibles, one finds at the end of the volumes a map recounting Paul's three missionary journeys.

Far from it, however, the history of the church and of the Christian faith does not begin with Saint Paul, and is not limited to his travels alone. The book of the Acts of the Apostles gives us a great deal of information about other figures who have made important contributions to the spread of the gospel around the world. Without dwelling on them too much, but without ignoring them, the second book of Luke relates to us numerous accounts that several commentators pass over in silence, captivated as they are by the detailed accounts of the Pauline missions, supported by numerous letters that he had sent to churches founded by him or by others.

The evangelists cited in the book of Acts are numerous. Among them, we can cite Peter, Barnabas, Mark, Stephen, Philip, Epnaetus, Lucius, Photina… and all the anonymous people who accompanied them or surrounded them.

The missionary journeys recorded in the New Testament begin with the command given by Jesus to go all over the world and announce the Good News of the Kingdom of God. Apart from the Twelve and the disciples who surrounded them, including the Seventy, Jesus prepared a man - of whom all the mysteries have not yet been explored - to play a key role, albeit discreet, in the evangelization and the founding of the first churches. This man was Simon of Cyrene, that same man who was forced to carry His cross on the road to Calvary, to Golgotha on the day of the crucifixion of the Son of God. He was the last makeshift companion of Jesus, who was left alive to tell us this story. The other two died on the cross at the same time as the Master.

Much has been said about Simon of Cyrene. And the late iconography depicts him sometimes as a muscular young man, sometimes as an elderly man with a long white beard. In other paintings he is dressed Roman or Egyptian, while in many of them he was depicted as a black slave. Some attributed the profession of carpenter to him, while others declared him to be a trader or winegrower. Yet the biblical text contains enough clues to enable us to describe it more accurately.

The story you are about to read tells the story of Simon of Cyrene and his spiritual heritage through his children and a friend of theirs, the Evangelist Mark. The information used is mainly taken from the New Testament, although it has sometimes been used, from secondary sources. You will discover why this North African was chosen to accompany Jesus to his place of execution, and how this experience served Peter, Barnabas and Paul, as well as others, to spread the gospel all around of the Mediterranean basin, from Cyrene in Libya, via Jerusalem in Judea, Antioch in Syria, Carthage in North Africa, Rome, capital of the Empire, Alexandria in Egypt, and to the ends of the Earth, Spain and Catalonia, ending in Avignon, in the south of France.

CANA

*I*t's party time in the village of Cana, in the Galilee! A wedding party. Seated around several low tables, many guests were dining. A troupe of musicians played famous songs, which people all over the region enjoyed. Stringed instruments, chalumeau, cymbals, everything to accompany these special moments where two beings will unite for life. Tradition exonerated the husband for two years from performing military duties. Two years during which the new couple would enjoy all the joys of marriage, possibly resulting in the arrival of a first child.

Young people were serving drinks to the guests. The cups, so far, were not empty. Unfortunately, the chief of ceremonies had not planned sufficient quantities of wine to satisfy all the guests. Calculation error, or unusual amount of consumption, always it had come to the point where the reserves were exhausted. A situation that disappointed the guests and made the organizer of the ceremony uncomfortable, not to mention the shame felt by the husband who did everything to make his party a success and that everyone left delighted with the evening. Some more guests, tipsy from the first cups, began loudly asking for more wine. Nathanael, being born and raised in Cana, was known to all. He hastened to calm the guests and reassure them of the availability of wine. He complained to the Master of Ceremonies.

John-Mark, uncomfortable with the situation, complained to his mother, Mary. The embarrassment was noticeable, and the organizers of the celebration had not prepared for such a situation. Then John-Mark's mother approached the other Mary, who had come with her children for the party. The eldest of her children was called Jesus, and he had stepped aside a little to appreciate the moments of conviviality created by this feast. Since the death of his father Joseph, he has become the first person in charge of the family. He had taken over his father's business in the carpentry industry. Two of his younger brothers supported him in this endeavor and the family has never wanted for anything.

Having heard what the other Mary had said to her, Jesus' mother hastened to tell her eldest son, whom few knew yet. She didn't know what to do to solve the problem, so she called on her son's talents, wits, or creativity to find a solution.

"My son, the wine is gone, and the evening is only in its midst. Our hosts do not know what to do to save our face in front of all these guests who ask for more," said Mary. *"I know you can find a solution for us. You've done this more than once, and in different circumstances."*

"Why are you telling me this?" answered Jesus. *"It would take a miracle to find wine at this hour. All the stalls are closed, and I can't go knocking on the winegrowers' doors so late to ask them to sell us wine. It would just take a miracle, and you know that my time has not yet come to make myself known to the world."*

Mary, remaining confident, made a sign to the servants who joined her. She said to them: *"I need you"*. And pointing to Jesus she added: *"Do whatever he tells you"*.

The servants looked at each other, and agreed to obey. Jesus, without saying a word, beckoned them to follow Him, and they went to the village synagogue, a few dozen meters from the place where the feast was taking place. Lined up against the wall, there were six jars of water, usually used for ritual ablutions and washings before entering the synagogue. The servants looked in, but they were totally empty. Jesus then asked them to fill them with water. They did so by going to draw water a few meters away, in the village well. Cana was not a big city, and we got around it quickly. All public amenities were close to each other. And after half an hour, all six jars were full.

The servants were now looking at Jesus, to see what he intended to do with all that water in the middle of the night.

He looked at the servants with a slight smile on his lips. *"Go,"* he said, *"and serve the guests. Fill their cups and come back to take more until all are well served."*

John-Mark, who had just arrived and who had attended the operation, wondered if this Jesus was really serious. What would the guests say if, instead of serving them wine, they filled their cups with water? It would be a shame for him, and above all, for the newlyweds.

However, the way Jesus had ordered to serve, he could not respond. The tone was both soft and firm. Imbued with a sort of authority, the words that came out of his mouth suffered no hesitation. And besides, the servants didn't need to be asked twice. Amused, they filled pitchers and poured their contents into the guests' cups, surprised themselves to see that the water they served had the color of wine.

A voice arose from the middle of the large table. A smartly dressed guest raised his voice and said:

"Usually at parties, we serve good wine first. And when people have had a good drink and are dizzy, we serve them a picket. I see that here you have done the opposite. You saved the best for last".

John-Mark, having taken a cup, tasted the wine served to the guests. He was surprised by the exquisite taste of the drink. He walked over to Simon and pulled him by the sleeve, whispering in his ear:

"Did you see what your master did? We filled these water jars ourselves. And now the water turned into wine!"

While keeping his voice low, Simon replied, *"It's a miracle! There is no other explanation."*

ACROSS THE GALILEE

*J*esus and his disciples traveled the Galilee, going from place to place, from village to village and from synagogue to synagogue. Jesus teached crowds and performed many miracles. The lame walked, the blind saw and the deaf heared. Several people bound by demons ware also delivered. When unclean spirits came out of the bodies, they often cried out, or begged Jesus not to torment them and allow them to go far away.

Jesus was surrounded by many disciples. Among them, Epnaetus of Carthage, John-Mark and his cousin Joseph, and Lucius of Cyrene, as well as many women like Joan, Salome, and several others bearing the widespread name of Mary, in addition to the twelve, those he called the Apostles.

Simon, whom Jesus had nicknamed Peter, was one of these twelve Apostles. He even seemed to be the most important of them, along with Andrew his brother and John, the son of Zebedee. Peter tells John-Mark not to stray from the group and to stay close to them.

"Thank you Peter," replied John-Mark. *"I feel good with you. I will always be near you. And Joseph too, by the way."*

A few days later, Jesus gathered his disciples together and asked them to get in pairs. The many disciples present each began to choose his companion, and sat down around Jesus. He chose seventy, then, with a smile on his lips, spoke:

"Go to all the towns and villages in the region. I send you out like lambs in the midst of wolves. Do not take anything with you. But in any house you enter, say first, "Peace to this house". Heal the sick who are there and say to them," The kingdom of God has come near to you. "Whoever listens to you listens to me; he who rejects you rejects me; and he who rejects me rejects him who sent me".

After that, the Seventy got up and set out two by two, in different directions, towards the towns and villages of the region. Mark and Joseph walked side by side. *"I am happy that the Lord has chosen us,"* said Joseph. *"What an honor for us! I was also surprised to have been chosen. Maybe it was Peter who told Jesus about me",* replied Mark.

"Yes, it is possible," resumed Joseph. *"He promised your late father to take care of you. He keeps his word. Let us thank the Lord for having been deemed worthy to serve him,"* added John-Mark. *"On the way back, my mother and I will go and settle in Jerusalem, not far from your property… If the Lord has no more mission to entrust to us. She just bought a big house there. We will be able to see each other more often".*

"I believe," continued Joseph, *"that we will still have to follow the Master. He has so much to teach us. I don't want to miss out on what he's going to do or say."*

"You are right Joseph. Me too. And I would like to go everywhere and tell these things. The world needs to know that there is still a prophet in Israel today. And even more than a prophet."

The two cousins then approached a hamlet, and went straight to the synagogue where a Torah reading was taking place. They came in and said, *"The peace of God be with you. Today the grace of God has reached us, and the Kingdom of God is among us. Jesus of Nazareth came from our God to destroy the works of the devil and do good to all who call on the God of Israel".*

Suddenly, a man gave a cry and threw himself on the ground, uttering threats against the two cousins. Then Joseph looked at him calmly and ordered the unclean spirit to leave that body in the name of Jesus of Nazareth. Another loud cry and the spirit went out. And John-Mark helped the man to his feet. The surprise was great, and the two strangers were invited to go to houses to deliver other people and heal the sick. The head of the synagogue welcomed them into his home, and together they commented on the scriptures to remind them that the times had come, and that God had sent his son to fulfill his promises to the children of Abraham. The next morning, Joseph and John-Mark left the hamlet, and went to other villages.

As if it had been programmed, the Seventy gathered around Jesus the same day, having returned from their mission. The disciples argued a lot among themselves and each related what had happened. The emphasis was on miracles that were done by their hands. Then Lucius, one of the Seventy, from Cyrene in Libya, spoke up and spoke to Jesus:

"Lord, we have accomplished the mission you entrusted to us with great joy. We have done many miracles as you commanded us. Even demons were submissive to us in your name."

Jesus, looking at him and addressing all of the Seventy, joined by many other disciples and people of all kinds, said:

"I was following you from afar, and I saw everything you were doing. And behold, I saw Satan fall like lightning from heaven. Here I have given you the power to crush snakes and scorpions, and to trample on all the might of the Enemy. Absolutely nothing can harm you. However, do not rejoice because the spirits are subject to you; but rejoice because your names are found written in the heavens".

CYRENE

$\mathcal{A}$ well-built man named Simon, in his forties, arrived at the port of Apollonia, dragging two donkeys behind him: on the first one, a woman was seated, while the second one was loaded with luggage. At his side, there were two young men in their twenties.

They unloaded the luggage and put it in a boat, while Simon helped the woman to get off her donkey. On the wharf there were also many people waiting to board with their luggage and goods. There were merchants, entire families and also, what appeared to be priests.

It had been a long journey from Cyrene. It was the start of spring, and the heat in North Africa was starting to heat up, as the landscape changed. The fields were green, and trees were greening again, while the roadsides were strewn with flowers of all kinds. It's the best season of the year. The birds were chirping and life was beggining to start again after a relatively mild winter. The Libyan coastal strip is relatively narrow, but well wooded and well exploited by the peasants who largely drew their subsistence from it. The fishermen were also well served, with a sea full of fish, while merchants of all kinds, from all over the empire, were happy to stop in this region for the most fruitful barter and trade.

There were several jars full of water in the boat, and the travelers needed them. Most travelers wore straw hats to protect them from the sun by day and humidity at night. A few of them were taking the boat for the first time, and seasickness awaited them around the bend. But the more experienced gave them advice to mitigate this effect mainly caused by the passage of the firm ground to the deck of the boat which swayed under the effect of the waves.

"Try to rest a little," said Simon to his wife and his two children. *"After a day of walking from Cyrene, we will have to regain our strength. We have three days by boat to arrive in Alexandria. Hopefully the sea is calm throughout the trip. There we will go to a hostel that I know before continuing our journey to Jaffa. So be careful and save your strength. You will see, Alexandria is a beautiful city. I don't know how long we're going to be there. Everything will depend on the places available on the next boats. I hope we don't have to wait long. Joseph is waiting for us for the start of Nissan for the preparation of the Passover. But don't worry, we'll have time to visit Alexandria and meet some interesting people there".*

What else to do in a boat for three days to pass the time? Simon engaged in a discussion with other travelers, while his wife joined other women chatting in the back of the boat.

"Is this your first time in Jerusalem? Simon asked one of the travelers. *"It's to Jerusalem that you're going, right? Just like me?"*

"No," replied the traveler. *"It's the second time. I went there for my Bar Mitzvah with my father. It was a long time ago. Today, I am accompanying my cousin who is convinced that we will meet the Messiah there".*

"May God hear him" Simon said. *"But we've been waiting for so long for His coming and also waiting for the final deliverance …"*

"According to an in-depth study of the prophecies," said another traveler, *"some say now is the time. But I cannot explain it. They have made calculations that are too complicated for me, and they are convinced that now is the right time."*

The expectation of the coming of the Messiah dates back to the time of Moses in the wilderness. He had announced that God would send from among the people a prophet like himself who would deliver Israel from all its bondages. This promise was confirmed to King David, when God promised him a descendant who would ascend his throne and reign forever. All the prophets have confirmed the coming of the Anointed One, and people have been attentive to all the signs foretold, in the hope of finding the exact date of his coming. The dispersal of Israel among the nations and the exile of Judah in Babylon only amplified this expectation of the Liberator, the one who would restore Israel. But since the prophet Malachi, a silence has fallen on the people, and no one has announced anything more. There is nothing left for the scribes and the doctors of the law, but speculations and calculations to try to find convincing clues as to the date of the coming of the Messiah.

ALEXANDRIA

*I*n Alexandria, Simon and his family stayed at an inn where there were already many Jews who had come from all over Egypt to take the boat to Judea. The Jewish community in Egypt was large, dispersed both in the Nile Delta and along the river in the towns bordering it. Simon had chosen this inn known not to serve as a place of debauchery. Because in this huge city, many hostels were used as places of debauchery. Especially those located near the port. Sailors liked to drink and sought the company of women of petty virtue. The evenings could end in orgies, a common practice among the Romans, or in generalized brawls. Naive foreign merchants, after having drunk too much, were also robbed and their stay could turn into ruin. A little closer to the city forum, the hostels were relatively quieter and better frequented. This is why Simon was relieved to see all these religious staying in the same inn as him, a sign of seriousness and security.

A Doctor of the Law with a long white beard, accompanied by a younger man, a heavy Torah scroll in his arms, arrived surrounded by many other people. He seemed to be well known, and people did not fail to greet him. Some came up to kiss his garment.

Once settled into the hostel, Simon, accompanied by his wife and two sons, went out to visit Alexandria. They first set off for the harbor and went back to admire the immense lighthouse that stood before them. They hardly could do it at their arrival. The legend considered it to be the tallest in the world. The structure was impressive, and many travelers stopped to admire it. At night, it could be seen from a distance of several stadiums, thus serving as a guide for travelers and a landmark for navigation. Then they returned to town and strolled through its vast boulevards. They looked at the forum, the temples, the theater, and went to the Synagogue. In Alexandria, you could meet people from different regions. Particularly from Nubia and Ethiopia.

"It was on this earth that the seventy-two sages translated the Torah from Hebrew into Greek," said Simon. "This country is renowned for having sheltered our ancestors from Abraham Avinou, the patriarchs and their descendants, until their deliverance by Moshe Ravinou who led them to the Promised Land".

"But Joshua got them out there, right?" Remarked the youngest of his sons.

"This is after an exile of more than four hundred years since God's promise to Abraham," the elder added.

"And how did we end up in Cyrene then?" Asked the cadet.

"It's a long story my son. I will explain all of this to you during the trip. We are Libyans, and our fathers converted to Judaism for so long that we have become both Libyans and Jews".

"*Alexandria looks a lot like Cyrene, but it's so much bigger and there are a lot more people,*" the elder pointed out. "*Even the architecture seems to be the same. With the name I bear, I feel right at home here*".

"*Children,*" the mom said, "*aren't you hungry? This visit has tired me a bit.*"

"*You're right,*" Simon replied. "*Let's go eat something, and make some provisions for the trip.*"

SEA

*D*uring the long journey to the territory of Judea, the travelers organized themselves to manage time, and to take advantage of it. The owner had arranged things so that everyone could find a way to withstand the vagaries of the crossing, despite the vagaries of the sea. Not everyone could take the boat, especially when it started to pitch. Again, some were seasick, and could be seen leaning out of the boat to empty their guts.

In a large hall inside, several people gathered around the Rabbi with the long white beard. On the large table placed alongside the cabin, a heavy Torah scroll was unfurled. The Rabbi then began to read and everyone was silent, listening with interest to what he was about to tell them. A few non-Jewish travelers looked at them in astonishment, and stood aside.

Simon and his two sons joined the group and quietly sat down to listen to the Rabbi.

"Since we have three weeks of travel ahead of us," said the Rabbi, *"we are going together to study all the texts of the Torah which announce the*

coming of the Messiah. So let's start with Bereshit. Right from the creation text, there is allusion to the coming of a savior because of Adam's fault ... According to a number of lawyers, the coming of the Messiah is scheduled for this season. A calculation made from the book of the Prophet Daniel would bring us straight to the present time. If this calculation is true, one should expect to meet the Messiah in Jerusalem. We will take advantage of this trip to verify all of this. Because indeed, he gave a schedule that spans seventy weeks. It would be weeks of years. And since there are seven days in the week, we have to consider the figure of four hundred and ninety years. And the calculation will have to start from the date mentioned by another prophet, Nehemiah. It begins with the publication of the decree of the Persian king, authorizing the Jews to return to Jerusalem after seventy years of deportation to Babylon, and to rebuild the city and the Temple. And that prophecy says that the calendar will be split in half. The second part concerns the end of times. It's the seventieth week. What interests us for the coming of Mashiakh are the sixty -nine weeks and their fulfillment. Now, if I'm not mistaken, the sixty-ninth week ends in our day. The Mashiakh should therefore not be long in showing up".

ORIGINS

*T*he wind is still fresh at sea, at the start of the season. But the bright sun softened the temperature on the deck of the boat. Simon and his wife, accompanied by their children, were sunbathing to recover from the cold of the night. Sitting on the aft deck, Alexander, their eldest child, struck up a conversation.

"Father, didn't you promise to tell us how our ancestors came to Cyrene?"

"Ah!" Simon looked at his wife and asked her to correct or complete it in his story.

"After the Flood was over," he began to relate, *"God told Noah and his children to scatter and fill the Earth. Each of his children took a different direction. Ham, the brother of Shem and Japheth, went south, and his son Puth crossed the Nile to settle in the territory of Libya. Some of his descendants have gone as far as the Pillars of Hercules, filling all the land west of the Nile. It seems that King Juba II, who died just recently, discovered islands which are located even further away, in the sea and which would also be occupied by the descendants of Puth".*

"Our ancestors, among whom there were the Libous, the Tehenou and the Temehou, have multiplied. And as time went by, they went further west of the land. Some have settled in the Pentapolis area. They mainly practiced agriculture and animal husbandry, due to the abundance of water. The Greeks say that there were up to three harvests a year there, and the ewes also gave birth three times a year. It was a rich and prosperous region. One day, Greeks arrived by boat, fleeing a terrible drought that had plagued their country for several years and caused them great famine. They were greeted by our ancestors who pointed out to them a well-watered place, telling them that there, the sky was full of holes. The migrants settled there, and built the city of Cyrene. They prospered and mingled with the local population and the many Jews already settled in the area. We ourselves are a mixture of these three cultures: Berbers by blood, Jews by faith and Greco-Romans by culture. The Greeks worked a lot and interacted with the natives. So our ancestors allowed them to settle in other cities, helping them to develop. This is how the Pentapolis developed."

"And what do you know about our family and our origins?" Rufus asked.

"What is certain," replied Simon, *"is that we are genuine Libyans. We have the same traditions, we speak the same languages as all the other Libyans, even at the Pillars of Hercules and throughout Mauretania. In our own family we have ancestors from all regions. We have given you a Greek name for Alexander and a Roman name for you, Rufus, while your mother has a berber name and me, I have a Jewish name despite my Africanity. But what matters is our devotion to our God and obedience to his commandments. And that's what we do by going to Jerusalem for the Passover."*

After a short silence, Simon continued, *"I have to tell you Jason's story as well. He could have been one of our ancestors."*

"Do you mean the famous Jason of Cyrene?" Alexander asked.

"Exactly," replied Simon. *"Jason of Cyrene. He lived about two centuries ago. He was a scholar who excelled in fluency in languages, especially Greek. After having studied in Cyrene then in Alexandria, he left for Jerusalem which was then under Greek occupation. There he realized that the Seleucid power was abusing its authority. Jason entered the administration and quietly took note of everything he witnessed. Before returning to Alexandria, he had amassed enough notes to begin writing a book. For that, he had to find peace and serenity which were greatly lacking in Jerusalem at that time".*

"But why? Rufus asked.

"King Antiochus Epiphanes had decided to impose Greek culture on the Jews. But he had met resistance and had failed in all his attempts, despite some success here and there. He realized that the heart of this resistance was in the Temple in Jerusalem, organized around sacrifiers and priests. So he decided to desecrate it in order to impose the worship of his idols on the Jews. Among other things, he installed a statue of Zeus in the square and sacrificed a sow to completely desecrate the place".

"Was he the one who caused the abomination of desolation? It's an event that has marked the history of Jews around the world, I believe", said Alexander.

"But how do you know that? Rufus asked.

"The Rabbi told us about it once in the Synagogue, at a party. But I was still very young, and I forgot the details of this story."

"This situation revolted a priest named Judah Maccabee. He led a revolt and despite the limited number of his supporters, compared to that of the

Greek troops, he succeeded in driving them out of Jerusalem and reclaiming the Temple. The first thing to do after that was to sanctify the place by cleaning it up and putting things back in place, especially the Menorah, the seven-branched candlestick that was never to go out. Unfortunately, there was not enough holy oil left to keep it alight. You could hardly light a single lamp for a day. Then the faithful, the priests and the elders began to pray, asking God to do a miracle, because it took eight days to make this oil. And the faith of these people was honored and their prayers answered. The only lit lamp had resisted until the oil was available again, and the other lamps could be turned on. A great feast called the Feast of the Dedication was held, and the Temple was again consecrated to the Lord. You know this holiday as Hanukkah. And we celebrate it at the start of winter."

"But," Rufus asked, *"what's that got to do with Jason? Did he take part in the revolt?"*

"Anyway," Simon replied, *"he witnessed it, since on his return to Alexandria he wrote a five-volume book in which he told the whole story. In many synagogues, an excerpt from this book, called the Book of the Maccabees, is read at every Hanukkah festival. This story is of great importance to the Jews, and it was told by one of ours, Jason of Cyrene. When we celebrate it every year, we often forget the role that Cyrene played in the transmission of that story".*

JAFFA

*H*ow happy the travelers were when the owner announced that they would reach the end of their journey the next day. It has been a long night, and Alexander and Rufus have stepped out onto the bridge several times to try and catch a glimpse of the shore. But that was only possible after the sun was up. Especially since at dawn, the mist covered everything that could be around the boat. And it was difficult to distinguish, a little later, the reliefs and mountains from the distant clouds.

The port of Jaffa seemed enormous to the two youg men. Nothing to do with that of Apollonia, yet already large, but less important than that of Alexandria, all the same. That of Jaffa was a connection for travelers coming from all over the Mediterranean to go to Judea or Galilee. Even if, for this last region, there was also the port of Caesarea located further north. The pilgrimages to Jerusalem, which take place three times a year, attract a large number of people, and trade has grown significantly in the region. If it were not for wars, frequent revolts and the permanent presence of the Roman army, the development of the region could have been done in an even greater way.

Tradition has it that Jaffa was founded by one of Noah's three sons, just four years after the Flood. Japhet, a few years later, would have taken the opportunity to bury Noah under a rock, after his death at the age of nine hundred and thirty. The name of Jaffa had been chosen by the brother of Shem and Cham, because it meant "beauty", so the site was so well located. The name of Japheth also descended from it. Suddenly, Alexandre and Rufus were captivated by the beauty of the place. The port of Jaffa was considered to be the oldest port in the world.

Travelers began to get off the ship once it docked. As soon as they got off the wharf, people approached them to offer their mount rental services. While the young men were bringing the luggage down with their mother, Simon was negotiating with a young man to hire two mules. On the first, he loaded the luggage, helped in this by his two sons, and on the second he helped his wife to get on. The road to Jerusalem was sloping, and it was going to be a long climb, for the city was on top of a mountain.

It was still barely a month since the Jews had celebrated the Feast of the Trees. Because very early on, the almond trees began to bloom, thus announcing the imminent arrival of spring. The people celebrated this feast to remember the blessings Israel received from God from the beginning. Three trees symbolized for them the grace of the Lord: the fig tree, the olive tree and the vine. Great celebrations were organized as soon as the first buds appeared on the almond trees, signifying that the harsh winter was over and that spring, whatever short, would soon set in. And this season is especially important spiritually, since it is at this time of year that God has instituted important feasts, including Pesach, Passover, one of the three pilgrimage feasts. This is why Simon of Cyrene took his family to the Holy City.

Mona, still concerned for the well-being of her family, reminded them to take some provisions for the road and to fill a skin with water.

"You are right," said Simon. *"The climb to Jerusalem will take two days. And we should take care not to exhaust ourselves".*

On the way, there were many pilgrims who took the same direction. All together, they formed like a convoy or a sort of caravan.

Simon entered into discussions with other pilgrims, while Alexander and Rufus got to know people of their own age. It was Alexander who initiated the discussion, addressing those who were right next to them.

"Where are you from?"

"From Rome!"

"From Rome?" Rufus said. *"It's so far, I was told."*

"Not that far," replied the pilgrim. *"Spain is even further."*

"Spain," Alexander added, *"is the end of the earth. It takes months of travel to get there".*

"I don't know," replied the pilgrim. *"I've never been there. I hope to visit it one day. But my dad doesn't like the idea. He says that in this country people raise pork in large quantities and export its meat throughout the Empire. But for us, pork is considered unclean. So we are not approaching it".*

"I would still like to visit this country one day," concludes Alexandre. *"There must still be some interesting things to discover there".*

JERUSALEM

*T*here were a lot of people in Jerusalem. It was through the crowded Jaffa Gate that Simon, his wife and children entered the city. People were almost on each other's toes. The way they dressed, you could tell where people came from all over the world. From Egypt, Greece, Cappadocia, Persia, Carthage, … and we could hear these people speaking foreign languages that neither Simon nor his family understood.

Fortunately, Hebrew was understood by all, and most wore the prayer shawl, like a uniform housing all men in the same boat.

Simon and his family walked through the City of David, passed the Temple, and stopped to admire it. The columns were majestic, and the stairs very high. Originally, the first Temple was built by Solomon. The Scriptures described it as a pure wonder. But over time Jerusalem has been attacked several times by foreign armies, and the shrine has been damaged quite a bit. When Herod wanted to restore it, he took the opportunity to enlarge it, especially as the population increased, the space often proved too small to accommodate so many pilgrims. In addition, it is said, Herod wanted to impress the Jews to push them see him as one of their own.

On the forecourt, it was like a kind of market. The bleating of rams and lambs could be heard, and traders talking aloud, each praising the quality of what he had to sell. According to the Law, people were to buy the paschal lamb four days before the feast. So everyone was eager to find one that met their desires or their means.

Simon, speaking to his children said how beautiful he found the Temple which he was also visiting for the first time. And he promised them that they would come back and visit it once they got settled.

"It is even more beautiful than the Temples of Cyrene and Alexandria," said Alexander.

"I agree," said his father. *"But now let's go to Joseph's. He must be waiting for us".*

Simon, Mona and their two sons arrived in front of a large house which overlooked a huge field. Cows, sheep and donkeys grazed quietly, while goats and billy goats hopped around. A busy man in the large courtyard adjoining the house put down his things and came to meet them.

"I guess you are Simon from Cyrene?" The man asked.

"Here are my wife and my sons, Alexander and Rufus," replied Simon. *"I take it you're Joseph?" We are glad to meet you".*

"Come with me, come in. You must be exhausted by this long journey".

"Oh, just a little. We couldn't wait to discover Jerusalem. It's been over a month since we left Cyrene".

It was Anna, Joseph's wife, who greeted the travelers from Cyrene.

"Joseph's cousin John told us all about you," she said. *"He is full of praise for you. I'm glad you're finally here. I will put you in your house. You will be comfortable there. Come on, it's just there behind".*

"John is like a son to us," Mona replied. *"When his family was in Cyrene, he played a lot with our children. But they had to flee the troubles in Cyrenaica, and we very much regretted them".*

CENE

*J*esus and his disciples joined Peter and John in the large room on the first floor of this important house which, it seems, belonged to John-Mark and his mother. The moment was solemn. A heavy silence reigned in the room. What was to be a festive meal suddenly turned into a moment of extreme tension. All of the disciples felt that something was brewing, and no one really had a heart for the feast. Did they read it on Jesus' face, did they understand it on their own?

Jesus opened the meal by sharing the cup of sanctification, after giving thanks. *"I praise you Lord our God, Master of the world, you who sanctify us by the fruit of the vine".*

The disciples shared the cup, drinking from it one after the other, then started their dinner. Silently. They didn't dare to look at each other, and everyone kept their noses in their plates.

It was Peter and John who did the service. While they were still eating, Jesus got up, took a loaf of bread, and gave thanks. *"I praise you Father, you who bring out bread from the earth".* Then he broke it.

"Take this," he told them, handing them the pieces he had cut. *"This is my body broken for you"*.

Each one of the disciples took a piece and ate it in silence. A few, however, were starting to look at each other to try and figure out what was going on. Why would his body be broken for them? They knew he had already said his body was bread. But they had taken it as an image to illustrate his speech. They never imagined that one day they would have to eat this bread as a real symbol of his body, and that it was going to be broken like one breaks bread.

They all went back to dinner without saying a word. But the unease was more and more noticeable. John sat down beside Jesus and leaned against him. Then the Master declared, to everyone's amazement, that one of the twelve was going to betray him. They looked at each other and wondered who it could be. It was excluded that it could be John, the favorite of Jesus, nor Peter, the first of the Apostles. It couldn't be James either, who was one of the three closest disciples to him. Nor of Judas, since Jesus seemed to trust him by making him responsible for the finances of the group. Even less Nathanael, whom Jesus himself said there was no fraud in him. Who could it be?

Still in shock, Jesus spoke to Judas and told him to go and do what he had to do. The latter took a piece of bread, dipped it in Jesus' plate and left, leaving the group to finish their meal with the Master.

The bitter herbs on the table were even more unbearable to swallow, and some of the disciples had difficulty finishing the meal. They were all relieved when Jesus took another cup, the second one, signifying that the Passover meal ceremony had come to an end.

"Here, drink. This is the cup of the new covenant. This is my blood, the blood of the covenant, which is shed for many. Truly I tell you, I will never drink of the fruit of the vine again, until that day when I drink it new in the kingdom of God."

The disciples drank, and began to sing the Psalms of Hallel, Psalms of circumstance that all the Jews sang during the festivals.

When dinner was over, Jesus and the eleven got up and went to the Mount of Olives, where they used to meet to isolate themselves from the hustle and bustle of the city. Night had just fallen.

At the bottom of the house, once the guests had left, John-Mark took a cloth, wet it and passed it over his body to cool off. He lied down on a bed, covered only with a sheet. The evening was hot, and heralded a summer that was going to be more of it. Fortunately for a few more weeks, temperatures could drop in the middle of the night.

As sleep began to take hold of him, he heard a noise outside, and voices that spoke loudly, but couldn't quite understand what they were saying. John-Mark looked discreetly out the window and saw Judas Iscariot accompanied by priests and soldiers, torches in hand. He then opened the window while being careful not to make noise.

"They must have left home by now," Judas said. *"But, follow me, I know where they've been. I'm sure they went to the Mount of Olives, to the Garden of Gethsemane."*

Mark, surprised by what he had just seen and heard, didn't even bother to get dressed. Only covered with the sheet he had on his body, he ran to inform Jesus and the disciples. But when he arrived at the scene, there was only the Master who had obviously just been arrested. There were no longer any disciples with him. The temple soldiers ordered Jesus to follow them, flanked by the chief priests and scribes.

John-Mark, having been discreet, began to follow them to see where they were going to take him. But a soldier saw him, and decided to walk around him to stop him. He grabbed the boy by the sheet wrapped around him, but the boy freed himself as he let go of the sheet. He found himself naked, and began to flee between the olive trees, taking advantage of the darkness of the night.

CROSS

*I*n Jerusalem, from the early hours of the day, an uproar arose around the Governor's House. A large crowd gathered in front of the Praetorium and awaited the verdict of Pontius Pilate, concerning Jesus whom he had just questioned and examined. After presenting him before the former high priest, Anna, he was tried by the Sanhedrin, under the presidency of the sitting high priest, Caiaphas. The subterfuges invented to convict Jesus were not enough to send him to the gallows, something the high priest longed for, to preserve his post. So he sent him to the Governor, who luckily was in Jerusalem that week at the same time as King Herod. The latter, after questioning him, contented himself with making fun of him and sent him back to Pilate, the only one authorized to condemn to death. But after questioning him in turn, he declared publicly:

"I find no crime in this man."

But the crowd demanded that Jesus be crucified. Fearing more uproar and turmoil, the governor has resigned himself to condemning the one he has just declared innocent. He washed his hands of it in front of the crowd, blaming the religious leaders who had brought one of theirs back to him, accusing him of wanting to be king.

After having him whipped and tortured, the Roman soldiers tied him to a cross, and led him to the place of his execution, crossing the whole city.

Jesus, bleeding, carried his cross and walked like a sheep being led to the slaughterhouse. The wood of the cross was heavy and Jesus had difficulty moving forward. All night long he had been questioned by his judges, then tortured before being handed over to Pilate who, in turn, had him beaten with rods. Jesus staggered, but got up. The Roman officer kept lashing him. He staggered and fell again a few meters further.

Along the way, a large crowd had gathered on both sides of the street. People were screaming. Some with pleasure, others with horror. Some rejoiced, while others lamented.

Coming back from the fields, after finishing his night shift, Simon heard the cries of the people, and walked towards the city. He made his way through the crowd, and found a man tied to a cross, staggering and falling, while the people were excited, with no one helping him. Everyone must have feared the Roman soldiers, when the man obviously lacked the strength to continue on the way to the place of his execution.

The Roman officer, desperate to get to Golgotha within the usual time frame, looked into the crowd, and saw this man, in his forties, well, covered in a cloak, obviously foreign to the region.

Addressing him, he ordered him to come over.

"You, where did you come from?"

"Fields," he replied. *"I kept the sheep there all night."*

"What's your name?"

Then the stranger replied:

"My name is Simon. Simon of Cyrene".

The officer therefore ordered him, forcing him, to take the cross of Jesus and carry it from there to Calvary, the place called Golgotha.

Simon of Cyrene pretended to resist. But he knew it was a waste of time.

The Roman officer took him by the sleeve and pushed him towards the cross. He gave him the threatening order to lift it up.

While Jesus was on the ground, Simon lifted the cross and put it on his shoulders. Jesus got up with difficulty, and lifted the cross with Simon, putting himself in front of him. The two men, the cross on their shoulders, walked towards Golgotha amid the cries of the soldiers and the howls of the crowd.

When they reached the place of execution, Simon placed the cross, looked sadly at Jesus, and left, knowing what was going to happen to him. Powerless in the face of this situation, he also knew he was powerless before the will of the Romans, and obviously, to the joy of the religious leaders and their accomplices who had followed the procession and were now standing at the place of execution, where two other men were already nailed to crosses. We can't wait for the coming of the Messiah to get rid of this foreign domination, Simon thought. "If Moses brought us out of the land of Egypt, land of oppression and bondage, It will be oppression itself that the Messiah must drive out of the Land of Israel."

SIGNS

Curious things happened on that day which started so badly for Simon. The man whose cross he carried must have been someone famous enough to have attracted so many people and mobilized both many Roman soldiers and several Jewish religious leaders.

Tired, Simon quickly went to bed to try to recover his strength and prepare for the celebration of the Passover whose dinner would begin at sunset. The boys weren't home, and Mona hastened to give him water to "wash his feet," and prepare him something to eat. Her husband must have been hungry after spending a night watching over the sheep. But Simon barely touched his plate and lied down on the big bed, falling asleep.

Around noon, Mona woke her husband who was sleeping deeply.

"Something curious is happening in Jerusalem today. The sun has eclipsed. This announces something not good".

Simon, still stunned by sleep, got out of bed anyway and opened the door to look outside. Indeed, a curious darkness enveloped the air, and an ominous silence reigned. Neither people nor animals could be heard making any noise.

"Where are the boys? He asked Mona.

"They went to see their friend John-Mark. They should be back soon. Maybe they'll tell us what happened?"

"I feel tired. I'm going back to bed. But don't worry. It must be just an eclipse of the sun. It doesn't last long".

Simon returned to his bed, while Mona returned to the door, anxiously awaiting the return of her children. But after a while, she remembered how much remained to be done for the Passover preparations. She quickly returned to her flour to prepare the unleavened bread. In Cyrene the preparation was a little different from that in Judea. As the quality of the flour was slightly different, the bread obtained did not yet meet Mona's requirements. In Cyrene, in fact, there were three harvests during the year. Between that of wheat, corn and barley, the choice of flour was extensive. And Mona knew how to vary the quality of her breads, both those called "unleavened" prepared especially for Unleavened Bread in the spring, and other types of bread the rest of the year … She also prepared a semolina pancake to accompany a summer dish, made with peppers and tomatoes seasoned with olive oil, which Simon grew in their garden".

The tradition of eating unleavened bread dates back to the very first Passover celebrated in Egypt, the day the Hebrew people left this country, towards the Promised Land.

Moses instructed the people to act with urgency. God's instructions on this matter were clear. The Hebrews were to prepare a Passover meal after having slain a lamb and brushed the jambs and lintels of the doors with its blood to protect them from the Angel of Death who was going to strike against Egypt that night. The Hebrews therefore had to be ready to leave the country at the signal of Moses. It was an absolute state of emergency, to the point where the meal had to be eaten while standing, and the men had to hold their sticks in their hands. The women didn't even have time to prepare the dinner properly, and had to bake the bread without giving the dough time to rise. Since then, and in memory of this event, Israelites consume unleavened bread as in the good old days, during the first celebration of this event. Later, the Law would specify that this consumption was to be done for a whole week.

The preparation of unleavened bread, called "Azim" bread, is very simple. Flour, salt and water. Its success therefore depends on the quality of this flour and the hands that knead it. And Mona wished she had the flour from Cyrene to make sure her bread was going to be of good quality.

Suddenly, in the middle of the afternoon, the earth began to shake. Simon woke up with a start, while Mona started screaming. Simon got out of bed and took Mona out of the house. The sun seemed to be gradually returning, but the emotions were strained.

Simon tried to reassure his wife, but she began to look into the distance, hoping to see their children return, while bringing her right hand to her chest.

"What's going on today Simon? First the sun which gives us false company, then the earth which begins to tremble ... I hope that all this only announces the coming of the Machiakh".

"I also ask myself the same question. Since this morning, I go from surprise to surprise. And I don't really know what to think anymore. Stay at home, I'll go get the boys".

"Oh no!" Mona said. *"You are not going to leave me all alone. I am coming with you".*

Mona quickly changed her shoes and put her shawl over her shoulders. Simon, meanwhile, walked around the house to make sure the walls hadn't cracked. He closed all the windows and the door, and knocked on the window of Joseph's house. It was Anna who opened, *"What's going on today? Joseph hasn't come home yet, and I'm very scared"*. *"Come with us,"* Mona suggested. *"We're going down town looking for the boys. Perhaps we will also meet Joseph there?"*

Along the way, Simon stopped to look at the houses around, and none seemed to have suffered from the quake. But Mona urged him not to stop, worried as she was for her two sons.

As they entered town, both parents saw their two boys coming home. Mona ran to them and exclaimed:

"My children, I was so worried about you. Are you ok?"

"Yes, we are ok, and I also believe that no one was injured in Jerusalem." Rufus replied. *"But we saw a curious gathering in front of the temple. I hope there was no damage there."*

"Have you met Joseph?" Anna asked. And as the boys were about to answer, Joseph called them from afar. He came hurrying up, knowing his wife was going to be worried.

"*Come on, let's go back home,*" said Simon. "*Our annual Shabbat is about to begin. Don't worry, I did the shopping on the way back home this morning. We are going to receive Epnaetus and Lucius for the meal*".

Just before nightfall, Joseph and Anna arrived, a wine jar in the husband's hands. "*It's some wine,*" he said when he introduced it to Simon who was receiving him at the door with his children. The couple were accompanied by two other young men.

Oh, thank you Joseph. So these are Lucius and Epnaetus you told me about? Come in, come in. It is nice to celebrate Passover with the family.

Rufus was the first to enter the house.

"*Mother, Joseph has arrived*".

Mona wiped her hands with a towel and introduced herself to her guests. "*Come in my children. What a joy to share the Lord's Supper with you. Especially with what we went through today. May the Lord keep us from all misfortune.*"

As Anna went to the kitchen to help prepare dinner, Epnaetus approached Mona and presented her with a gift.

"*It was not necessary, my child. You have to feel at home. Thank you so much.*"

"*It's a pleasure, Mother Mona. I met merchants in town who came from Carthage. This is where I was born and raised. So, I thought you would like this tablecloth*".

"Are you from Carthage?" Alexander asked. *"I have always dreamed of visiting it. In Cyrene, we were told that there were two cities to visit in his life: Alexandria and Carthage. After Jerusalem, of course".*

"And Rome," Lucius added. *"It is the capital of the Empire. You have to visit it at least once in your life".* Then he added: *"Here for you is a vial of perfume that came straight from Antioch. I am happy to offer it to you".*

"Oh, how generous you are. I am really touched. Thank you so much. Children, give them water to wash their feet. The meal will be ready in a few minutes".

Joseph, realizing that Simon had not said a word since their arrival, asked him:

"I have the impression that you are a little tired Simon. Was yesterday's vigil complicated?"

"No, not at all," replied Simon. *"It is always a joy to see lambs coming into the world. I had a very pleasant evening. I look tired, but in reality it was what happened after, when I got back home that shot me down. When I got back from the fields, I heard the sound of a shouting crowd coming from the city. I walked over to see what was going on, and here the Romans were leading someone to Golgotha. He had been made to carry a cross on his shoulders, and it was evident that he had difficulty in carrying it. His body was bloodied. Certainly he had been beaten with rods and even tortured. The Roman officer who was in charge of the execution forced me to carry the cross of the unfortunate man to Calvary. My heart was torn to see how this man was being treated. Despite all of this, he stood up and joined me to carry his cross with me. He wanted to wear it himself. And if he could, I think he would have done it on his own. When I got to Golgotha heights, I dropped the gallows there, and left in awe. I will never forget this man".*

"Yes, it's not a normal day, I admit. I too heard people screaming. Then there was an eclipse of the sun, then an earthquake ... So, I quickly forgot those screams and expected something else to happen to us again. "What's going to happen again? I asked myself".

"We heard about it, but I didn't know you carried that cross," Alexander said. *"Also, a lot of people preferred to go home quickly for fear that something might happen to them. Passing in front of the Temple, there were many priests in front of the Parvis. They all seemed to be restless. I wonder what happened. We looked for John, but we couldn't find him. I wonder where he's gone. We did not dare to go look for him at his place."*

"John told us about this Jesus. He spoke highly of him to us, and we have been to the Temple these past few days to listen to him. Even the Doctors of the Law could not stand up to him. He had answers to everything, and avoided all the traps they set for him. When I left, I heard two scribes say that they had to get rid of him at all costs."

*"Enough of the gossip my children. The meal is ready,"*Mona interjected.

"Thank you very much for all these wonders, Mother Mona. May the Lord reward you a hundredfold."

The table was well stocked. Joseph, being from the tribe of Levi, that of the priests, was attentive to the respect of the commandments and the traditions. Everything was there: the main course, the lamb, the bitter herbs,...

Simon poured the wine brought by Joseph into a cup and recited the Kaddish.

"Blessed are you, Lord God of Israel, Master of the World. May your Great Name be glorified and sanctified in the world. May you establish your kingdom, make your salvation flourish, and hasten the time of your Messiah, in our living and in our days and in the days of all the house of Israel, as soon as possible … May great peace from Heaven, as well as a good life, and satiety, and salvation, and comfort and safeguard, and redemption and forgiveness and atonement, and relief and deliverance be granted to us and to all Israel … May he who makes peace in the heavenly spheres extend it in his mercy among us and throughout all Israel, amen!"

PASSOVER

The next day, Passover Day, thousands of people from all over the world gathered in and around the Temple square for the solemn celebration of the Passover.

The people, covered by their prayer shawls, avoided looking at each other.

"This is not the kind of Passover I was hoping to celebrate when I came to Jerusalem. Look at how sad people seem," said Simon.

"Even the priests and the scribes avoid looking at people. You can tell they're upset about something," Alexander replied.

"It's certainly because of this Jesus that they crucified yesterday," Rufus said.

"Hush," Simon said. *"Don't say that name in front of these people. We don't know how they might react. Come on, the service is over. Let's go back* home".

On the way back home, as the crowd dispersed, Rufus remarked to his father how disappointed he was with the ceremony. *"Even in our synagogues in Cyrene it was happier."*

"There," Alexander interrupted, *"we all knew each other. There weren't all these crowds from everywhere. What is impressive though is both the splendor of the Temple and the number of pilgrims".*

"Tomorrow, if you wish," said Simon, *"you can come with me into the fields to pick the sheaf of wheat".*

On the third day, as Simon and the children had gone to the fields to collect the sheaf of wheat and carry it to the priests who officiated in the Temple, as the Torah requires, John-Mark, panting, knocked on the door of the house of the Cyreneans.

"Good morning Mother Mona, are Alexander and Rufus there?"

"No my child, they went out with their father".

"What's going on? I see that you are very out of breath".

"Do you know about this Jesus who was crucified last week? He is risen!"

Without waiting for Mona's reaction, Mark ran away. He walked out of town, towards the fields where Simon was working.

Simon, Alexander and Rufus and a few other servants were busy in the fields, when John-Mark had arrived panting.

"Do you know what happened? Jesus is risen!"

The two brothers turned at each other in astonishment, then looked at their father.

"What?" Simon said. *"That same Jesus that I accompanied to Golgotha? Risen?"*

"Yes, himself! He appeared to women, then to his disciples. You have to come and see".

The two brothers looked again at their father who shrugged in disbelief and nodded to them. They hastened to follow their friend.

"Along the way, we will pass by to inform Joseph as well. He must be made aware".

Arrived in town, Joseph, John-Mark, Alexandre and Rufus, went to the house of Mary, the mother of John- Mark. A servant opened the door for them.

"Enter my children," said the hostess. *"We are living an exceptional event and joy floods this house".*

There were already several people in the large room on the ground floor. People seemed excited, and there was heated discussion. Despite their excitement, many remained in disbelief at such news.

Suddenly, Mary sang a song, and everyone fell silent to listen to her.

"Sing to the Lord! Dazzling is his glory …"

Then everyone began to sing along with her.

The news quickly spread around town, and opinions differed on the subject. Many didn't believe it, and some even laughed at those who reported it. *"How would a man be resurrected after three days in the tomb?"* They said.

Some went to the Temple to consult the scribes and the doctors of the Law. Among them, no one seemed to give the rumor any credit. Unless…

One of the scribes quickly went to tell the high priest about it, busy with the rituals of shaking the sheaves of wheat, after having sewn up his priestly robe which he himself had torn during the questioning of Jesus. Seeing the signs the scribe was giving him, he knew there had to be an emergency. He therefore took advantage of a respite during the ritual to discreetly receive the scribe.

"There is a rumor going around the city that this Jesus who was crucified three days ago was resurrected".

"This is absurd," replied Caiaphas.

"The tomb is empty, and the soldiers in charge of its protection say they saw nothing, and do not explain how it could have happened. It will run in all the streets and in the houses. And we risk having new troubles. We must act quickly and hush up this affair".

"And do you have any idea how to do it?"

"If you will allow me Caiaphas, I will spread another rumor to say that it was his disciples who stole the body of this Jesus, to make it appear that he is risen."

"Excellent idea. Anyway, there are no other explanations. Go, and I will confirm this before the Council".

RESURRECTED

*I*n Mary's house in Jerusalem, the apostles were gathered around a meal, and told how they saw the risen Jesus, in a house and on the road to Emmaus, …

"We didn't recognize him, so he walked with us for a long time, telling us how the scriptures announced his death and resurrection. At one point we begged him to come home with us. At mealtime, he gave thanks. It was there that our eyes were opened and we recognized that it was indeed the Lord. He then explained to all of us, from Moses and the prophets, how the prophecies were to be fulfilled, that the Messiah was to suffer and then be resurrected, and how they were fulfilled in his person".

As everyone listened to Peter, suddenly Jesus appeared. Everyone was surprised, and everyone was amazed. Peter didn't need to say more. The Lord, the Master was right there among them. And Jesus to invite himself to their table.

"Peace be with you! He told them.

But no one dared say anything back. He sat down among them, took the bread, gave thanks, and began to eat with them, the bread and the fish that Mary had prepared. He showed them his hands and feet, and the point on his side, proving to them that it was indeed him, still bearing the stigmata of his crucifixion.

Jesus was indeed risen and there was no longer any doubt about it. Everyone wondered what would happen next. Would he also show himself to the world, to the priests and to all who had crucified him? How would Pilate and the Romans react if they suddenly faced evidence of the resurrection of the one they had put to death a few days earlier? And if the appearances of the master would be reserved for them only, how would the world react upon hearing the news, and how would they convince him of it?

So many questions that the Master would answer in the following weeks.

Jesus appeared to them several more times, for forty days, reminding them of his teachings and explaining their mission to them. Then on the fortieth day, having all gathered on the Mount of Olives, he appeared to them again, and began to give them specific instructions:

"Do not leave Jerusalem, but wait to receive what the Father has promised you. You're going to receive power when the Holy Spirit comes upon you; then you will be my witnesses in Jerusalem, in all Judea and Samaria, and to the ends of the earth. Go through everyone and proclaim the Good News of the Kingdom of God. Baptize those who believe, and pray for the others".

Then, with these words, he was taken up into heaven under the gaze of his disciples.

WRAP

*T*hat evening Joseph invited Simon and his family, Epnaetus and Lucius to his home for dinner. Anna, his wife, had prepared fish for them with vegetables, in the manner of the Cypriots from whom Joseph came. Cyprus is an island located off Greece and Syria. But for ages, it had also received populations from other parts of the world, such as Italy, Spain, Israel, Egypt and Libya. It is no wonder that the Cypriot culinary tradition is a mixture of all these other traditions, whose heart is linked to the sea. But descending from the tribe of Levi, one of the twelve tribes of Israel, Joseph knew how to distinguish between fish permitted by law from those that are prohibited. Generally, Moses classified animals into two categories, those that are eaten and those that cannot be eaten. And he had shown the characteristics that made an animal be considered food or not.

Epnaetus, himself from Carthage, was already thinking of the celebration of the Feast of Weeks, called Pentecost. It takes place every year after seven weeks following the feast of the Firstfruits, where the sheaf of the harvest is presented to the Temple. Pentecost then kicks off the harvest season, and all of Israel is busy reaping the many blessings that God has bestowed upon the people through the produce of the land. Moses, did he not say that the Promised Land was the land of wheat, barley, vines, fig trees and pomegranate trees; land of olive trees and honey. The purpose of the presentation of the wreaths was to ask God for his blessing to obtain a good harvest. After the harvest, each one brought to the House of the Lord a tenth of what he had obtained from the fields. It all took place in an atmosphere of anticipation and celebration. The disciples of Jesus had therefore agreed that on the occasion of this feast, they would meet in the house of Mary, mother of John-Mark in Jerusalem, to await what the Father had promised them. But they didn't know where, when, or how it would happen. Jesus spoke of the deep things of the Spirit, not the forms they would take. Moreover, to Nicodemus, the Doctor of the law who had gone to see him in secret to try to understand the mysteries, Jesus replied that the Spirit came like the wind. We do not know where he came from or where he is going. Peter and the Apostles did not know either. They just encouraged the other disciples to obey the Lord's command and trust Him.

"In a few days the feast of weeks will take place," said Epnaetus to Simon. *"We are going to meet in John- Mark's house. Will you be with us?"*

"Alas, no," replied Simon. *"We will still be in Jerusalem, but will be spending the party with an old aunt that we wish to visit before we return to Cyrene. But the boys will certainly be with you".*

As he climbed to the top of the hill, Simon admired the reflection of the sun on the wheat field he was tending. With the breeze, it looked like a golden lake whose gentle, light waves were blown by the wind. The lambs born two months earlier had grown well. Some will soon be ripe for adulthood, and will in turn become capable of procreating and securing new litters for the following springs. Sheep's milk fed the lambs, and was also used to prepare nutritious cheeses sold in markets in and around Jerusalem. Simon took a deep breath as he felt the joy of the work done. Soon he would be returning to Cyrenaica, and will certainly have a lot to tell there, of his stay in Judea and Jerusalem. He figured he should be able to come back to it later. Maybe to end his days there. Especially since he realized that the climate of Cyrenaica and that of Judea were not that different, and that around Jerusalem there were many people from his country. There is even a so-called synagogue of the freedmen, attended mainly by people who came from Libya, after having been freed from Roman slavery.

SPIRIT

*T*he House of Mary was large. She lived there alone with her son John-Mark, and a maid. When she and her husband arrived from Cyrene, accompanied by their young son, they had first settled in Galilee, before deciding to sell everything to live in Jerusalem. They believed that their place should be near the Temple, especially since they belonged to the tribe of Levi, whose vocation was the worship service.

But since the arrival of the Romans a century ago, everything has been turned upside down in the way the cult works. Even the Sanhedrin had seen its prerogatives reduced, and many priests had had to seek work to meet their needs. And the Lord had been generous with John-Mark's parents, who were abundantly blessed. Therefore, the house that was bought in Jerusalem was so big because, they had thought, they would consecrate it to the Lord. However, throughout the Empire, the Romans were careful not to interfere in the religious affairs of the conquered populations, except when they used their temples as bases to organize the rebellion against Rome. So the governors and proconsuls exercised a sort of control over religious activities, but did not go so far as to prohibit them.

Since the death of her husband, Mary has opened her house to needy pilgrims and to all those who need a place to stay or a roof for a few nights. John-Mark grew up often seeing foreign visitors to his home, and the Lord never abandoned them.

This Pentecost eve was also going to see a lot of people flock to the house, especially since on the ground floor there was a very large room capable of accommodating dozens of people. The family maid had already cleaned everything, as usual, she expected to receive pilgrims for this feast. And it was no surprise that by the end of the day, she saw people arriving at the house. She already knew some of them, including Peter and John, and a few others. She understood that their visit was not a request for lodging, but that it had another purpose. Dozens of other people, men and women, flocked to the house, and Mary received them all, as if she knew them personally. John-Mark, joined by Alexandre and Rufus, chatted with most of them, in a good-natured atmosphere. They were all disciples of Jesus who had come as if to look for something. Among them, distinguished fishermen, traders, peasants, priests,... as well as the Apostles whom all seemed to identify clearly.

Songs had suddenly started to be sung. First, the songs of the Hallel, songs for the occasion that the Jews sang on certain feasts such as Passover or Pentecost.

Sometimes songs were interrupted by the reading of a passage in the scriptures, especially those relating to the coming of the Messiah. They sang Psalms and prayed all night long without a break.

The next day, when the Sun was now high in the sky, and the pilgrims outside were going to the Temple for morning prayers, suddenly there was a loud sound of strong wind in the house. All present looked at each other and looked around. Flames of fire arose on each of them, and all, men and women, big and small, began to speak in various languages: Greek, Latin, Berber, Arabic, ...

Everyone present left the house and went to meet the crowd who were looking for where the noise was coming from.

This one was more and more numerous, and the disciples kept praising God in all languages to the surprise of the people who arrived in greater numbers.

Then a man in the crowd spoke aloud to make himself heard:

"We come from all over the world to celebrate the Feast of Weeks. From Rome, Asia, Egypt, Cyrene, Cappadocia, Mesopotamia, and all parts of the earth. But you come from Galilee. How is it that each of us hears you praising God in our own dialect, in our mother tongue? Have you lost your mind? Did you drink early in the morning?"

"What is happening has been announced by the prophet Joel," replied Peter: *"It will happen in the last days, says God, that I will pour out my Spirit on every creature: your sons and your daughters will prophesy, your young men will have visions, and your elders will have dreams. Even on my male servants and my female servants I will pour out my Spirit in those days, and they will prophesy. I will do wonders above in the sky, and signs below on the earth: blood, fire, a cloud of smoke. The sun will be turned into darkness, and the moon will be turned into blood, before the day of the Lord comes, a great and manifest day. Then whoever calls on the name of the Lord will be saved".*

Quickly, many pilgrims gathered around the apostles and were baptized alongside the inhabitants of Jerusalem who were happy to finally understand, who was this Jesus who had come to them and whom they crucified. Hundreds of people came to the spring of Siloë where there was a large pool of water to be baptized. The number of people who had passed through the waters of baptism that day was estimated to be some three thousand.

Obviously, Rufus was at the height of his joy. In the streets of Jerusalem, with Alexander and Mark, they roamed the streets to announce the Good News of the Kingdom, and the number of people who believed increased day by day. Despite his youth, he did not hesitate to speak to old people to tell them that Jesus was the son of God, the true Messiah of Israel. Every evening, they gathered in the temple around the apostles and listened to their teachings. Many people would bring food or money and give it to the apostles in order to provide for the needs of all who came, especially the widows and orphans who were thus cared for.

The children of Cyrene felt that the world had changed and that henceforth everyone would be converted and accept that Jesus was truly the Messiah announced by the prophets. There was no longer any distinction between the origin of the pilgrims. All were considered as brothers, equal before God and before men.

Day after day, as the number of people from Judea came to the temple to listen to the apostles, the number of pilgrims dwindled. One after another returned home after participating in the Feast of Weeks celebrations and witnessing the harvest of souls for the kingdom of God.

The family of Simon of Cyrene was also due to return to Libya, to resume their ordinary life totally disrupted by their experience in Jerusalem, and to have witnessed exceptional events. The boys were eager to tell their story to their buddies in Cyrene, and Mona had already made the list of women she was going to visit to tell them about her experiences in the holy city.

LIBYA

*B*ack in Cyrene, Alexander and Rufus as well as their father went from synagogue to synagogue and announced the Good News of the fulfillment of the Law and of the Prophets. The Jews who had not been able to make the trip to Jerusalem this year listened with interest to the pilgrims' tales.

"We have told you our testimony to convince you that Jesus is the Messiah, the Son of God, and that by believing you have forgiveness of your sins. Yes, the Messiah came as the prophets announced. God has kept his word and we are witnesses of it. Get baptized in the name of the Lord Jesus, and receive the gift of the Holy Spirit. This is what we will also preach throughout the Pentapolis after having toured Cyrene: Berenice, Arsinoe, Apollonia and Ptolemais".

Simon of Cyrene spoke and recounted his experience with Jesus. He assured his audience that everything in the scriptures is consistent with what has happened in recent months in Jerusalem. *"Hundreds of people saw him after his resurrection, and many even ate with him. He ascended to heaven and announced that he was going to prepare a place for us there and come back and get us so that we could be with him forever.*

You realize, we are also going to meet our Father Abraham, Moses, the prophets and all the righteous men there," he added.

"When I lifted the cross of Jesus, I only thought I was helping a poor wretch to pay for his sins. Now I understand the words of the prophet Isaiah. "But who believed what was announced to us? Who has recognized the arm of the Lord? He rose up before him like a weak plant, like a shoot coming out of a parched ground; He had no beauty or luster to catch our eye, And his appearance had nothing to please us. Despised and abandoned by men, Man of sorrows and accustomed to suffering, like one whose face is turned away, we have scorned him, we have taken no account of him. However, it is our sufferings that He has borne, it is our pains that He has taken charge; and we considered him to be punished, smitten by God, and humbled. But he was wounded for our sins, broken for our iniquities; the punishment that gives us peace fell on him, and by his stripes we are healed. We were all wandering like sheep, each one followed his own way; and the Lord has laid iniquity upon him all of us. He was mistreated and oppressed, And he did not open his mouth, like a lamb which is brought to the slaughter, Like a sheep mute before those who shear it; he did not open his mouth. He was taken away by anguish and retribution; and of those of his generation, who believed that he was cut off from the land of the living, and slain for the sins of my people? His sepulcher was placed among the wicked, his tomb with the rich man, although he had not committed violence, and there was no deceit in his mouth".

"The disciples of the Lord were gathered on the day of Pentecost," Alexander added, *"when suddenly a loud noise like the wind was heard, and tongues of fire rested on their heads, and each one of them they began to speak in other languages, praising God in all the languages of the world, in fulfillment of Joel's prophecy, surprising pilgrims from all over the world. Disciples in Galilee also began to speak our own language of Libya. We are*

witnesses to it. Thus, the Comforter that our Heavenly Father had promised was given to us that day".

A man among the participants in the meeting intervened and insisted on giving his testimony.

"I am a trader, and I travel a lot. I was in Jerusalem on the Feast of Weeks, and I visited the Synagogue of the Freedmen, where many Jews and God-fearing from Cyrenaica meet. On the day of Pentecost, I was present in the courtyard of the Temple when one of Jesus' disciples, a certain Simon called Cephas, spoke to the people explaining how God kept his promises by sending Jesus as the Messiah. I was convinced of his speech, and saw hundreds of people convert and be baptized that day. I did the same, and I also encourage you to believe in this Messiah and to be baptized".

Simon spoke again and added: *"This Good News must be announced throughout Libya, and in all neighboring territories. We will have to make sure that all our brothers receive it. In synagogues, in fields, in public places and in markets. For it is written that whoever calls on the name of the Lord will be saved".*

Following in his father's footsteps, Alexander spoke in his turn: *"In the next few weeks, I will take the road to Tripolitania to make sure that in the synagogues the Good News is announced. We will start by going around the Pentapolis and we will announce it to Apolonia, Ptolemais, Berenice and Arsinoë. I will be accompanied by brothers from Libya near Cyrene whom I met in Jerusalem during the Passover and the Feast of Weeks. We will go to Oea, Leptis and Sabratha, and throughout the region. God willing, we will continue our journey to Carthage. It should also not be forgotten that many of our brothers are established in Cyprus. If there are those who wish, they can accompany my brother Rufus who plans to be there soon to testify to the goodness of our God".*

From day to day, from Sabbath to Sabbath, Rufus roamed the synagogues of the region to bear his testimony. In one of them, and after reading the Torah, the rabbi invited Rufus to Take.

"As we were in Jerusalem for the Passover feast," Simon's younger son said after greeting the congregation, *"we witnessed something extraordinary. Back from the fields where my father, Simon of Cyrene watched over the sheep, he was requisitioned by a Roman officer to take the cross of a man condemned to death. He later found out that it was Jesus of Nazareth whom the Jewish religious leaders and the Romans decided to crucify because he foretold that the Kingdom of God was in our midst and that the times are fulfilled. Three days later, when he was buried in a tomb guarded by soldiers, these disciples, some of whom we knew, announced that he had risen and appeared to the women who had gone to visit his grave, then appeared to them again several times. The tomb was overcome by the power of God. It is this Jesus whom God chose to proclaim his word according to what he promised to Moses, saying "I will raise up for them a prophet like you from among their brethren, and I will put my words in his mouth, and he will speak to them. whatever I order from him". It is this man whom God has chosen to bring salvation to everyone who believes. Repent for the remission of your sins and get baptized. This is the message that I will also preach to our brothers in Antioch, that it is Jesus who is the Lord. Several brothers from Cyrene will accompany me there, and I hope that there will also be some of you who will want to come with us."*

ANTIOCH

 $\mathcal{A}$ few weeks later, Rufus and a few others gathered in the Antioch synagogue on a Sabbath day. The service was conducted under the leadership of the rabbi who insisted that only the Messiah had the power to save. Recalling the Lord's promises to Abraham, he traveled through the history of Israel, showing that Jesus was that Messiah. Obviously, the Good News touched many Jews in the region.

At the end of the service, Rufus heard a voice behind him: *"Who do I see there?"* He turns around and finds himself facing Lucius. *"What are you doing in Antioch?* Lucius and the travelers hugged each other.

"You stay breaking bread with us, aren't you? Lucius asked.

"With joy," Rufus replied. *"So you will give us the news of the brethren and tell us what you too are doing here?"*

"I imagine you are aware of what happened in Jerusalem recently? There was a wave of persecution. Stephen was stoned, and we had to flee to find shelter. Only Cephas, John, James and a few others remained there. A young

rabbi from Tarsus lashed out against the Lord's disciples, throwing them in prison and encouraging their stoning".

"But tell me, what did you come to do in Antioch, and what becomes of your parents, and your brother Alexander?"

"My father and mother stayed in Cyrene", Rufus replied. *"Father has resumed his work, and is busy spreading the Good News throughout the Pentapolis. He hopes to return to Jerusalem one day. My mother supports him tremendously by visiting women and sharing the gospel with them. As for Alexander, he went to Tripolitania, hoping to reach Carthage later".*

"Carthage?" Asked Epnaetus. *"I also plan to be there soon. Maybe I'll find him there?"*

The next day, Rufus, accompanied by several other people, went to the city forum. As in all cities of Greco-Roman culture, the Forum is the place where most people meet. It was the place where news was exchanged, and projects of all kinds were developed. A place of conviviality and discussion, it was also the right place to engage in public debates on issues of concern to society. Rufus and his companions took the opportunity to approach people and initiate discussions.

Speaking to a Greek man, Rufus began to discuss their way of greeting each other with him. Because in fact, instead of simply greeting each other, they uttered an expression which affirmed that Caesar was lord, like the other divinities: *"You worship several divinities and you call them Lord? Do you know that in truth there is only one Lord? He lives in the heavens and he came to visit us to tell us that God does not reject people, but that in every nation he who fears him and practices righteousness is pleasing to him".*

"It is Jesus who is Lord, and it is only through him that every man can obtain salvation. Men have not been given any other name by which we can be saved. In him we have life, movement and being".

The Greek was surprised by this statement and tried to answer it, as the crowd surrounded them. A heated debate ensued on the matter, and several people stayed to learn more and urged Rufus and his companions with questions.

That evening, at Lucius's home where Rufus and some of his companions were invited to settle, the discussion ensued around the proclamation of the gospel in the region.

"It's wonderful how many conversions there are in this town," Lucius said. *"Jews and pagans are converted every day and ask for baptism".*

"And the movement is going further and further, to the most remote villages," Epnaetus added. *"Wherever the word is spoken, people answer the call and obey the Lord."*

From now on, the inhabitants of this rapidly expanding city, enriched by the silk trade, elevated to the rank of provincial capital by the Romans, considered that a new community was born within it. It included a good part of the population evangelized by brethren from Cyprus and Cyrene. To designate them, people gave them a name: Christians.

*"I notice that the synagogues are full, and many God-fearing and pagans are joining the Lord. You have to organize yourself to be able to support and teach them,"*suggested Rufus. *"No matter what name we are given, we know that we are children of God, members of the body of Christ. We carry his message, his life and his hope. We are only Men, and have nothing*

special that would distinguish us from others. Our works and our actions will speak for us".

The following Sabbath, during the synagogue service, the rabbi welcomed *"people from Jerusalem."*

"Let me introduce to you brothers who have come from Jerusalem to inquire about this sudden wave of conversions in our region. I invite Joseph, who some know as Barnabas, to say a few words to us."

Barnabas rose from the crowd, to the astonishment of Rufus who had not recognized him on the first try.

"May the grace of God and the peace of our Lord Jesus Christ be with you. We heard in Jerusalem that great things are happening in your area. The apostles and the elders charged us to come to you to realize for ourselves the extent of the grace of God which has been granted to you. God having spoken to the fathers of old in many times and in many ways through the prophets, has spoken to us in these latter days through the Son, whom he made heir of all things, by whom also he made the universe, and who, being the radiance of his glory, and the imprint of his being, and upholding all things by the word of his power, after having purified from sins, sat at the right hand of the majesty, in the high places; having become so much more excellent than the angels, that he inherited a name more excellent than theirs. I look forward to meeting you all, to the joy of God. We are at your service to support and encourage you".

After the service, as Barnabas was surrounded by several people urging him with questions, Rufus called him.

"Joseph, I am happy to see you again".

"Rufus, what a surprise!" Barnabas said. *"God is filling me with his joy. I am so happy to see you again. What happens to your parents and your brother Alexandre?"*

"My parents are in Cyrene, and Alexandre went to announce the Good News in Carthage via Tripolitania. I haven't heard from them for some time. It won't be long before I return to Cyrene to find them. But in the meantime, I will show you around the region to get to know the new believers. They will be happy to meet you".

Going from place to place, from village to village, making the rounds to visit the believers in the area, Barnabas, Lucius and Rufus were chatting with people. Barnabas always found the right words of comfort and encouragement. *"Persevere and proclaim the Good News of the Lord Jesus around you. God extends his grace to all and invites all men to repent and to live in righteousness. Remember to take care of the widow and the orphan, and help those in need find a new path in life."*

After returning to Lucius' house in the evening, Barnabas continued to urge the brethren:

"Through his Son Jesus Christ, God has visited us and extended his grace to us. Let's make sure that no one is deprived of it. Let's not forget our elders and work diligently".

"Blessed are the meek, for they will inherit the earth, as the Lord has said. Blessed are the merciful, for they will find mercy. Do not return evil for evil, but do good without getting bored of it. Let us be patient and compassionate, and let none of us think of taking revenge on anyone, for vengeance is on the Lord. If someone falls, let's help them get up. Let us pray without ceasing, and raise clean hands to the Lord to praise him. Let's walk together so that we can go even further. And the peace of God

which surpasses all understanding will guard our hearts and our thoughts in Jesus Christ".

The next morning Barnabas spoke to Rufus: *"I looked forward to meeting all these new disciples. In view of the grace that has been granted to this city and the number of conversions, I must go to Tarsus in Cilicia to find someone who will be very good to meet all these brothers and sisters. I am sure he will be surprised to see how the Lord has stretched out His hand on the Gentiles. So I will be away for a while".*

"Don't worry," Rufus told him. *"There are people here who can handle the situation. Lucius and the elders of the church will know how to ensure that no one is deprived of the grace of God. Even the number of churches is growing. Precisely, while Epnaetus is going to Carthage, I will take the opportunity to visit my parents in Cyrene. We will meet again, God willing, when you return".*

PARENTS

It was a long trip and the seas were quite rough. It was necessary to stop several times on the way, because the ship going to Cyrenaica was also carrying cargo that it had to deliver to different ports. He took the opportunity to disembark some travelers as well and to embark others. Those who were to continue their journey took the opportunity to go down to dry land to stock up in the port stalls for the rest of the journey. But in the end, the crossing was done without too much hassle.

So Rufus landed in the port of Apollonia not far from Cyrene, which was further south, inland. He found the horse rental company, but just took a mule on which he put his things and which he mounted under the scorching sun.

After a day of travel, he saw the suburbs of Cyrene. He returned to his hometown and bypassed the Forum, the theater, the temples dedicated to Apollo and Zeus, the statues,... People seemed busy, and no one was paying attention to him.

Arriving near his parents' house, Rufus was recognized by neighbors who had come to greet him. Children accompanied him to the doorstep of Simon and Mona's property, happy to see a stranger coming to visit them.

Rufus pushed open the garden gate and entered without knocking. The inner courtyard has not changed. He knocked on the interior door and shouted, *"Father, mother!"*

Mona left the house, quite moved to find her son. *"Rufus! God be praised. I am so happy to see you again".*

They fall into each other's arms.

"I am here, mother. I have not forgotten you. You are still so beautiful and in good health, as far as I can see".

"I'm so happy to be with you again. Where is father?"

"Your father works a lot. But today he's home because he's a little tired. Come home, you will surprise him".

Upon entering the house, Rufus looked around and noticed that nothing had changed. At the same time, a lot of memories came back to his mind. He was born in this place and grew up there, together with his older brother, Alexandre. Neighbors their own age would join them there and share a lot of things together. The table in the middle of the main room could testify to the number of times it welcomed them to learn to read and write, play and eat together, under the supervision of Mona or Simon, when he returned from the fields.

Rufus looked around for his father, but couldn't find him. *"Father, are you there?"*

"Is it you Rufus my son?" Answered a voice from the back room.

"Yes, it's me father. I missed you both, and I came back to visit you and mother."

Simon left the room and Rufus hugged him. *"How are you?"*

Mona interrupted them. *"You must be very thirsty my son. Here is some fresh water and some lemon. What long journey have you made?"*

"Yes, tell us, where did you come from?" Simon asked after taking a sip of water. *"The last time we heard from you, you were in Cyprus".*

"I come from Antioch in Syria. It was there that the Lord led me with many other brethren, and we proclaimed the Good News to the Gentiles. God is doing great things there. I met Joseph there. He has instructed me to convey his greetings to you".

"Joseph is a good boy, isn't he?" Said Mona

"Absolutely! He is full of wisdom and I always appreciate his presence. He knows how to say the right words at the right time."

Simon and Rufus went out into the garden of the house. The son saw some effects of age on his father, but said nothing about it.

"Have you heard from Alexander?"

"Yes," replied Simon. *"He writes to us from time to time and sends us news with the travelers who come to Cyrene. He is now established in Carthage. This is where the Lord seems to have called him there. At first he worried us a little about your mother and me. He wanted to travel around the world to announce the Good News, and we prayed a lot for him".*

"He first went to Tripolitania and stayed there for a while. Time to help establish communities and teach them in the ways of the Lord. Then he went to Numidia and to the Getulia. Today there are communities of believers in all these regions: Lambesis, Tamugadi, Cirta, Calama, Hippo, Saldae, Caesarea ... And even as far as Tingis, Anfa and Volubilis near the Ocean. The Lord is proclamed everywhere and many people are baptized. And I'm not telling you about Carthage or it's downright spectacular, I was told, despite the shackles of the Roman governor. The number of churches there keeps increasing."

"Before leaving Antioch," said Rufus, *"Epnaetus told me he was going to Carthage. He will surely meet Alexandre. I'm sure that will make him happy. And here, how is it going?"*

"Many people have turned away from pagan practices and turned to the Lord," Simon replied. *"Many believers have opened their homes to welcome disciples and hold meetings. Our old synagogues can no longer contain all these people. From time to time there is lively discussion about the person of the Lord. This is mostly caused by those of our brethren who do not believe that Jesus is the Messiah and are still waiting for the coming of the Savior of Israel. But it doesn't go any further, and the atmosphere is peaceful. It's good".*

"What about you," Rufus asked, *"what's happening to you in all of this?"*

"At my age, I have reduced my activities a lot. I don't travel that often anymore. I just encourage the brethren, teach and help the elders in their work. They are often together, sharing meals, studying the scriptures, and persevering in the way of the Apostles. The grace of God can be read on their faces, and they are a true blessing to the whole region. Even the governor consults them on the most delicate questions in the management of public affairs."

"Come to the table!" Mona shouted from inside the house. *"You will be able to eat and chat quietly. That way, I could also take advantage of it".*

Simon and Mona spent the evening listening to their younger son recount his stay in Cyprus and Antioch. The next day, Simon and Rufus went to town and walked between the Forum and the amphitheater, not far from the temple of Zeus, *"almost as imposing, it is said, as that erected in Athens"*, as did notice Rufus to his father. *"How I would have liked to have seen my people turn away from this paganism and believe in the living God!"*

"This is what we all want here. We pray for this regularly. I will introduce you to the community, and you will be able to meet our brothers and see how the church here is growing," Simon replied. *"But first, I wanted to talk to you about something, but not in the presence of your mother. I don't know how long I still have to live on this earth before going to join the Lord, if he doesn't come back by then. I would like to entrust your mother to you, in case I have to go first. This is also what the Lord had done with his mother, entrusting her to his disciple John".*

"Listen to me, Father," Rufus replied. *"I don't even know if I won't be the first to go. The Lord decides, and there is no need to worry about it. If he decides to call one of us back first, you can be sure he has already prepared something to take care of those who are left after him. Be at peace. I will never abandon my mother. Neither you. I will take care of you whatever the circumstances".*

The two men entered a house located a few steps from the Forum. Many people were gathered in a large room. They sang Psalms. Quietly, Simon and Rufus found places and sang along with the others.

After the chanting ended, a person who seemed to be the owner of the place asked Simon, *"Who is this person who is with you Simon? Don't you introduce him to us?"*

"This is my youngest son, Rufus," replied Simon. *"A lot of people here already know him and his older brother, Alexandre. He returns from Antioch with great news. We should listen to him."*

The master of the house motioned to Rufus and invited him to speak.

"Great is the Lord, and great are his works," Rufus began to say. *"Brothers left here for Antioch. They stopped along the way and took other people from Cyprus with them to speak the word to the pagans living in Syria."*

"The grace of God was then extended to the Greeks and the God-fearing, making many converts. We can no longer count the number of baptisms of people from all over the region, to the most remote villages. So much so that the brothers in Jerusalem heard about it and sent Brother Joseph to confirm what they had been told".

"Today Jews and Gentiles walk side by side in the way of the Lord. The number of disciples is growing day by day. And I see with joy that here too the number of disciples has increased and that now the whole region believes in the Lord. It is said everywhere that brothers who have left here are announcing the Good News wherever they go. It is a matter of joy and pride for me to see that my compatriots show so much zeal for the Lord".

The Cyreneans were interested in the experience of Antioch, especially with regard to the pagans. Because the Jews already had the Torah and the Prophets as models, while the pagans entered into an unprecedented experience.

"We had to adapt our speeches in form, without giving up on substance," Rufus replied. *"For example, regarding the Messiah, the Gentiles had no idea who he might be and what his role would be in the history of salvation. The notion of Christ to them didn't make much sense. We must have told them more about the Lord than about the Messiah. Because they know what a Lord is. It was then necessary to explain to them that the only Lord is Jesus of Nazareth. For at the same time that he is Lord, he is also the Son of God. He was sent by God to save mankind. This speech was clearer to them, as most of them know nothing about the history of Israel and the prophecies."*

SAUL

*I*n Antioch, Barnabas was back. He was accompanied by a man younger than him. He was about thirty-five. Welcomed by the brothers, he introduced Saul as a rabbi who met Jesus after having persecuted him. *"I knew him in Jerusalem, and I introduced him to the apostles before he returned to Tarsus. I'll leave it to you, Saul, to tell how you met the Lord,"*said Barnabas.

"I don't know how to say how happy I am to be with you. My name is Saul. I was born in Tarsus in Cilicia, and studied the scriptures at the feet of Gamaliel in Jerusalem. All my life I have been zealous for the Law of God and have fought against all those whom I considered to be heretics. This is what I did with the Lord's first disciples in Jerusalem. I put several of them in jail and even approved of their stoning to death. In my zeal, I requested letters from the elders to go and arrest the disciples who were in Syria. And it was on the road to Damascus that I met the Lord. Suddenly, a dazzling light came and blinded me and I fell to the ground. I heard a voice saying to me, "Saul, Saul, why are you persecuting me?". So I asked, "But who are you Lord?" And the voice answered "I am Jesus whom you persecute". I remained blind for three days. And in Damascus, the Lord sent me someone

who prayed for me, and I regained my sight. I was baptized then, and I began, in all the synagogues to teach that Jesus is the Son of God. Brother Barnabas came to fetch me from my home in Tarsus, and it is a grace for me to be among you. I look forward to listening to you and learning more with you, about the Lord and his mysterious ways."

Saul had quickly integrated into the community of Antioch, and never missed a reading and meditation session. He worked in parallel to earn a living by making and selling tents. He diligently followed the teachings of Barnabas, deepening his knowledge of the Law of Moses and the fulfillment of the prophecies concerning the Messiah in the person of Jesus.

While they were praying, a man came and knocked on the door. Lucius opens. *"Agabus! What a joy to find you again. Come in!"*

"Unfortunately, I'm not bringing good news. I come from Jerusalem. The Lord showed me that there was going to be a great famine throughout the land of Eretz Israel."

"We must then thank the Lord for informing us in advance," said Barnabas. *"Let us organize to collect donations from the brethren all over the region here, and take them to Jerusalem."*

This should be done as quickly as possible. That's why everyone got involved right away. The church appointed three people to receive the donations and keep track of them so that the whole operation would not suffer from any ambiguity or misunderstanding. Day after day, those responsible for the collection were accountable to the elders of the church, until the amount collected was sufficient.

BOARDING

*O*n the port of Apolonia, Rufus and his parents boarded a boat bound for the Island of Crete opposite Libya. Apolonia was the landing place for the Greeks who had come a few centuries earlier to find refuge in Libya, fleeing the drought and famine that raged among them. It was considered to be the port of Cyrene, located about twenty kilometers further south. The development of the port was somewhat hampered by the founding of Alexandria a few centuries later. The latter city grew so important that it had become one of the three most important Roman cities, competing with Antioch.

In this season, the sea was rather calm, and the winds were favorable. The trip was shaping up to be good. Especially since the boat was going to Crete, which would make it possible not to spend too much time at sea. But the Cretan stopover was not going to be long, and it would be necessary to take another boat to continue the journey towards Jaffa. This detour would avoid the trip to Alexandria, located rather in the east, when the goal was to reach Jerusalem as soon as possible.

"We will get to Jerusalem quickly", Rufus said. *"I think that Mark and Mary his mother will welcome us without any problem. I left Joseph in*

Antioch on his way to Tarsus to bring back a brother who will be useful for the ministry, he told me. In addition, I forgot to tell you, he sold one of his fields and gave the fruit to the church to take care of the needy".

"Glory to God!" Mona exclaimed. *"This brave Joseph really is a good person. I enjoyed him very much the whole time we were at his house".*

"That's true," Simon added. *"He always thinks of others. He is at their service. As a Levite, he knows that his only share, his only inheritance, is the Lord. So he relies on him. I find him both humble and courageous".*

"I learn a lot when I'm with him. In Antioch he was giving teachings on the scriptures, and I must admit that he has a very thorough knowledge of them. The brethren drink his words as if they were from Christ himself. But he never boasts about it, if he even takes the lead. He is much appreciated by all, and also, very well respected. People know that he also has the confidence of the Apostles."

FAMINE

When they arrived in Jerusalem, Barnabas, Saul and their companions realized how severe the famine was on the people of Judea. Along the way, they had observed the decline in people's activity. The businesses were almost all closed, and there were a lot of poor people on the roadsides. Sadness could even be read on the faces of the priests they passed along the way. At one point Barnabas and Saul were even tempted to begin distributing their help along the way. But at the last moment, they decided, as originally planned, to hand over all the donations to Jerusalem church leaders, which would distribute them, because only them knew the real needs and the really needy.

Jerusalem smelled of sadness, and even in the public squares there was no more only the poor who did not even have a roof over them to shelter. Because many were forced to even sell their houses in order to be able to buy some food. Many residents have also had to leave the region to seek refuge in Samaria or the Galilee. Others have gone as far as Lebanon, Syria and Even Egypt.

Several famines have been reported by the biblical texts. As for example, that which had raged for three years during the reign of David. Or again, that lived in the time of the prophet Jeremiah. He said that sometimes he had to go through the trash cans to find something to eat.

Simon Peter quickly brought together the Apostles and the Elders, so that they could see what their brothers in Antioch sent them. In the court of the Temple in Jerusalem, Barnabas spoke to Peter, John, James and the elders: *"We have brought back gifts from the brothers of Antioch to our loved ones in Jerusalem. In addition to these gifts in money and in kind, the brothers assure you of their constant prayers"*.

"Glory to God"! Peter exclaimed. *"And thank you to all these brethren. The elders will handle the distribution wisely, according to individual needs. I'll call John-Mark to give them a hand. He is a great resourceful person on whom we rely a lot"*.

MARK

*R*ufus and his parents walked towards Mark's house. Inside, there were a lot of people. It was Mary who welcomed them with a big smile: *"Welcome into the house of the Lord. Every time you come, I feel the grace of God that fills this house even more"*.

"You too are a great blessing to us Mary," replied Mona. *"How is our beloved John?"*

"Always at the service of the brothers. He doesn't stop running," Mary replied with some pride. *"Despite the difficult times we are going through, he never stops crisscrossing the city, helping the most disadvantaged. If it was not by the grace of God, I believe that nothing would have been possible"*.

In the great hall were Barnabas, Saul and several other people.

"What a surprise you are giving us!" Mark cried out. And Joseph got up to take Simon in his arms. *"Joseph is henceforth called, Barnabas by the Apostles"* added Mark. *"Here is Saul of Tarsus, and these are the other brothers who came with me from Antioch"*.

"I am happy to see you again Simon and Mother Mona, as well as Rufus". Barnabas said. *"All that's missing is Alexander to fill my joy. I hope that when you are rested, you will accompany us to Antioch? As for you, John, we are very happy with the work you have done in distributing aid to the needy here in Jerusalem. I would be happy to have you with us, and certainly Saul too, because in Antioch too there is a lot to do".*

Mark glanced at his mother who nodded. For in Jerusalem he is also very useful. Especially since the house of Mary was open to the service of the brethren. But she lacked nothing. She had a maid and the brothers were always there to help, especially since they saw Mark's mother as a mother to them as well.

"It will be a joy for us to join you later in Antioch," Rufus added. *"We will stay here awhile first, then do as the Lord leads us. Father is a little tired at the moment, and he will need more time to rest".*

BARNABAS AND SAUL

The Church of Antioch included people with gifts and talents. There were Doctors, Prophets, Evangelists, and the Elders of the Church had taken care to encourage them to meet regularly to pray together and consult on important matters relating to the proclamation of the Good News, while they took care of the day-to-day management of church affairs.

In the house of Lucius, there were Prophets and Doctors gathered to fast and pray together in search of guidance from the Spirit for the work of the Lord. There was that day Barnabas, Simeon called Niger, Lucius of Cyrene, Manahen, and Saul.

While they were praying, Manahen addressed the small assembly and said, *"I feel the Holy Spirit is saying to set Barnabas and Saul apart for the work to which he has called them."*

"Indeed", added Simeon, *"I too feel the same thing"*.

"I also confirm," Lucius said.

So Barnabas could think of nothing else to add and said, *"May the will of the Lord be done, here in Antioch or wherever he wants to lead us ..."*

And Saul concludes with an *"Amen!"*

So Simeon, Manahen, and Lucius got up and laid their hands on Barnabas and Saul. *"Lord, you who know everything and who can do everything, we entrust our brothers Barnabas and Saul to your grace and ask you to accompany them wherever you send them to announce the Good News to peoples and nations. May signs and wonders be done by their hands, and the nations to see your power through them. "* begged Lucius.

CYPRUS

A few days later, Barnabas and Saul, accompanied by John and other disciples, boarded a boat heading for Cyprus.

"I know Cyprus well," said Barnabas. *"I was born and spent many years there. We will get there soon. I know a lot of people in the area. We will find them all at the Synagogue during the Sabbath Service".*

"I can't wait to meet them. And also to discover what the Lord has in store for us as surprises", said Saul.

Even traveling light, there was some luggage to deal with. And Mark took care of it.

As usual, Barnabas and Saul, accompanied by Mark and a few other brothers, went to the Synagogue on the Sabbath day. They had gone down to the port of Salamis and Barnabas had shown his companions around the city. At the end of the service, the head of the Synagogue gave the floor to Barnabas. *"I come back to Salamis and to my country, accompanied by Saul and my cousin John, whom some must already know. We are witnesses of the Lord's grace and his faithfulness. What he promised to Abraham, then through Moses and the Prophets, was fulfilled in Jesus of Nazareth, the Messiah. He came to tell us that the time has come for the Lord's visitation, and to open the way to the Lord, so that through him we may receive the remission of sins"*

Many miracles were done by the hands of Barnabas and Saul, and the multitude surrounded them. Which made a lot of noise in the city. Many sick and infirm were brought to the synagogue, and they were healed immediately, and the name of the Lord was glorified throughout the region.

As they left the Synagogue, a Roman officer approached Barnabas: *"Proconsul Sergius Paulus begs you to honor his invitation and come to his palace without delay. He wants to listen to you".*

Barnabas looked at Saul, Mark, and their companions. *"It will be with joy. Let's go".*

"Please follow me," said the officer. *"He was told on your speeches and the miracles you do."*

The proconsul Sergius Paulus received the three companions with great warmth. He told them what he was told about them, and expressed his desire to listen to them himself. He needed to understand the mysteries of God. *"I made you come to hear you myself. It has been reported to me that you are announcing a new doctrine throughout the island of Cyprus, and that by your hands great wonders are done."*

But, among the counselors of the proconsul, was a magician named Bar-Jesus, son of Jesus. But people called him Elymas, because that meant, wizard. He feared for his place, scaring that the newcomers would win the heart of the proconsul and be engaged in the palace. *"Don't listen to them excellent Sergius,"* he said briskly. *"These people want to stir up trouble and turn you away from your faith in the Roman gods."*

The wizard's intervention irritated Saul, whose name has just been changed to Paul, like that of the proconsul. He therefore spoke, thus anticipating Barnabas, to respond himself to the governor's request.

"We thank you excellent Sergius. It is by grace, by means of faith that every man is called to turn away from evil and to turn to the true God. He sent his only begotten Son to save anyone who trusts him. He calls every man to turn away from evil and to do good".

But Elymas did not intend to stop there: *"It is heresy that these men preach, Excellent Proconsul. No one can be saved from the wrath of the gods that way".*

Saul, continuing his speech undisturbed by the magician, continued by declaring: *"Never before has salvation been so near. It is given free of charge to anyone who believes".*

But Elymas continued to interrupt Saul who was growing more and more irritated. He felt his spirit boil inside him and feared that the proconsul would be influenced by the magician who said, *"I beseech you Excellency. Don't listen to this man. He says crazy things".*

Then Saul, using his spiritual authority, addressed the magician and said: *"Man full of all cunning and deceit, son of the devil, enemy of all righteousness, will you not cease to pervert the righteous ways of the Lord? Now, behold, the hand of the Lord is upon you, you will be blind, and for a time you will not see the sun".*

Immediately the sight of Elymas disappeared. He went blind instantly, in front of everyone and groped for people to guide him. The proconsul, seeing what had happened, approached Barnabas and Saul. *"I believe. What should I do now?"*

"Turn away from all evil and be baptized for the remission of your sins," Paul told him. *"And the God of grace will keep your heart and your mind in Christ Jesus."*

Paul, feeling winged after the experience with proconsul Sergius Paulus, took matters into his own hands and decided to lead the mission himself, instead of Barnabas who said nothing and let him do it. *"Let's go to Pamphylia to announce the Good News there,"* he said to his companions, to whom he added others he had met on the spot.

After a short crossing of the sea by boat, Paul, Barnabas and their companions disembarked at Perge. Mark, who had not said anything since Cyprus, gave Barnabas a questioning look. It was not to be that way. The Holy Spirit appointed Barnabas first, as Peter did in Jerusalem. There was no question of handing over the leadership of the mission to Saul who, in addition, changed his name to possibly match that of the proconsul of Cyprus.

Mark took Barnabas aside and, taking precautions not to hurt his cousin, reminded him that he had been appointed as head of mission, and that it would be wrong to let Saul take the reins. *"Look, we are in Perge, and he decides to go straight to Antioch in Pisidia, without even trying to announce the Good News here, in this city, and without even consulting anyone. Not even you"*. But Barnabas tried to reassure him by telling him that God was in control anyway. *"No, Barnabas, you shouldn't say that. Not only is Saul not showing respect to you, he is also not even concerned with respecting the order given by God. In my opinion, he will be facing big problems and he might train you with him. Be careful and try to channel him a little, for your own good and for his. This mission is yours, and don't take the risk of letting it fail. Saul is younger than us and he doesn't have your experience."*

"The mission is incumbent on all of us. I remind you that you are in the same mission as us".

"I regret cousin. I cannot continue with you under these conditions. I'm going back home. I cannot bear the disrespect that this dear brother shows towards you, and ours too, by changing the initial order of the mission without consulting anyone. I've been thinking a lot since Cyprus. I am returning back to Jerusalem."

CIRCUMCISION

While Mark had left for several days in Jaffa to go to Jerusalem, Paul and his companions found the brothers in Antioch and recounted their journey.

Paul spoke to some of the brothers who had come to listen to them and related: *"Everywhere we went, Cyprus, Antioch in Pisidia, Lystra, Iconium, Derbe, the hand of the Lord was with us, and many miracles have been done through our hands, and there have been many who have come to the Lord. Unfortunately, several of the disbelieving Jews created problems to us, going so far as to drive us out of their cities or even stone us. But the grace of God allowed us in the midst of all these trials to announce the Good News anyway, and many were converted"*.

Lucius spoke up, taking advantage of the pole that had been handed to him. *"Precisely, in this regard, and in your absence, several people among our converted Jewish brothers have come from Jerusalem and are causing trouble among the brothers. It is urgent to take things in hand"*.

The next day, Barnabas, Saul, and several others met with the brethren who had come from Jerusalem and discussed the points of contention to try to clarify matters. Lucius had made them well aware of the situation, and Paul thought he would sort things out quickly. But the discussion was heated, and no one seemed able to respond convincingly to the challenges raised by the disciples from Jerusalem. One of them, speaking of the converted pagans, said: *"If the Gentiles are converted, they are welcome, but they will have to be circumcised according to the rite of Moses. Otherwise, they cannot be saved"*.

Barnabas, whose word was respected by the brothers in Antioch, intervened in the debate, although he had been silent from the start. *"Salvation in the Lord Jesus is obtained by grace, by means of faith. There is nothing more we can add to it. Circumcision is a sign of the Covenant that the Lord made with Abraham Avinu. But it is not circumcision that saves"*.

Paul added, *"If you think circumcision saves, then Christ died in vain."*

But the brother from Jerusalem returned to the charge declaring: *"In Jerusalem all are circumcised. You can check it with the apostles"*.

Then Barnabas spoke again and suggested, *"Why then not go to Jerusalem and consult with the apostles and the elders? If you want, a few of you can come with us. At least we will have a clear answer on this subject"*.

PAUL

*I*n Jerusalem, Mark found his mother Mary as well as Peter and his wife Strapola and the brothers he had left there before his departure for Antioch.

"Didn't you know what happened to Cephas"? Mary asked her son. *"He was arrested and put in jail. For several days, there was a wave of persecution that surprised us,"*she added.

"So what?" Mark asked, looking at Peter.

"The Lord intervened in a spectacular way, to the point where we had a hard time believing it," Strapola replied. *"God has sent angels to prison to set him free while we were gathered here to pray for him. And when he came back the evening after his release, we couldn't imagine he was knocking on the door. What a joy it was to see him again. Since then, the authorities have left us in peace".*

"Mark looked at Peter again, and I rejoiced that he was released. Then it was Peter who asked:

"So how are things going in Antioch?"

"We experienced great things in Antioch. Many people come to the Lord, to the point where the population now identifies us with the name of Christians. This shows that the gospel message has become public and that there are no restrictions on its dissemination. Besides, the Holy Spirit asked to set him apart Barnabas and Saul. So they went on a mission to Cyprus, and they asked me to accompany them. There were many conversions and the Lord extended His grace to those who wanted it. Even Proconsul Sergius Paulus accepted the Good News and was baptized".

"The Proconsul himself?" Peter asked. *"Glory to God. Even the governors are touched now. That's excellent news".*

"Yes, indeed," said Mark, whose expression had suddenly become sad. *"But from there, something happened, the reasons for which I still don't understand. Barnabas led the mission from the beginning, according to the word of the prophets given in Antioch. But just before going to Paphos, Saul had his name changed and now he is called Paul, like the proconsul. Since then, he was the one who made the decisions without asking anyone for advice. He therefore decided to take us to Perge, but did not see fit to announce the Good News there. He wanted to go to Antioch in Pisidia, without even stopping in the towns along the way. So I told Barnabas, who had not reacted to these changes, that I preferred to return to Jerusalem, and that I could no longer continue with them under these conditions. I needed to consult you on this to find out what I should do."*

"When I see Saul again, I will thank him," exclaimed Mary. *"Because he allowed me to find my son, whom I had not seen for a long time."*

"I'm glad to have found you, too, mother. You know, I still miss dad".

Mark's statement surprised his mother. *"Who would not miss Aristobulus? I think about him constantly. But he is with the Lord, and I rejoice for him"*.

"He always reminds me of King David," Peter interrupted them. *"He bravely faced the lion to save your life Mark"*.

"It's true, and the Savior of the World then saved my father. This experience made him discover who really was this Jesus whom I invoked every day".

COUNCIL

*O*n the city, the news of the arrival of Barnabas and his companions soon spread around Jerusalem. The church, the Apostles, and the elders gathered to listen to them, and Barnabas reported the testimonies of what God was doing in Antioch and the area. The brethren in Jerusalem praised God for what they heard from the mouth of Barnabas. Then, the latter came to the reason for his trip to Jerusalem with his companions:

"With Saul and several brothers from Antioch, we have come to consult you on a question relating to the obligation or not, for the pagans to be circumcised according to the rite of Moses."

Some of the Pharisees who have been converted have found it obvious that circumcision is mandatory and have made it known. *"They must be circumcised and made to observe the tradition of Moses,"* they declared.

But the Apostles and the elders, aware of the divisions that this question may provoke, decided to withdraw to treat it in serenity.

After a lively debate between them, Peter took the floor to suggest a step of wisdom, rather than answering with a *"yes"* or a *"no"*. *"You all know how it was through my mouth that the pagans first received the Good News. I am of the opinion that we do not impose a yoke on them that neither we nor our fathers were able to bear."*

"I am therefore of the opinion that one does not create difficulties for those of the pagans who are converted to God, but that we write to them to abstain from four things", added James: *"the defilements of the idols, the fornication, strangled animals and blood. For the rest, we must remember that for many generations Moses has had people preaching him in every city, since he is read every Sabbath day in the synagogues. It would be wise to listen to him".*

Thus, the question of circumcision had to be put in context, and not be treated separately. For it was to Abraham that circumcision was given as a sign of the Covenant, between God and the descendants that he was going to give him, beginning with Isaac … not to Moses. The latter indeed established a rite of circumcision for his people. But he was not the initiator of the Covenant itself. Regarding the rite, the Apostles considered that it should be treated in accordance with the teachings given every week in the synagogues where the Law of Moses and the texts of the Prophets are read precisely. The Law was clearly more important than the tradition.

Peter spoke again and proposed to write a letter to the church of Antioch and to have Barnabas and Paul accompanied by Jude, called Barsabas and Silas, themselves prophets, to give them the explanation.

Did the Apostles do this on purpose, or is it due to the secrets of God? Mark felt that the choice of Jude and Silas was an extraordinary mystery. Because, being a multilingual, Mark knew how to switch from one language to another, from one meaning to another. Jude was nicknamed Barsabas. A name close to that of Barnabas. Whereas

Barnabas means son of consolation, Barsabas means son of rest or son of return. In the scriptures, Judah saved Joseph's life when their brothers threw him into a well and let him die. Joseph owed his brother his life. Now Jude or Judah vouched for Joseph, called Barnabas, to the community of Antioch. Like a fair return of history. As if the circle had just come to close. But it was the same with Silas who had a Latin name, whose Hebrew equivalent is Saul. Mark saw clearly that by a mystery which exceeded him, this mission which the Apostles had initiated in the direction of Antioch was doubly covered. Especially since the letter they wore on behalf of these Apostles was intended for the city of Antioch and the entire region of Cilicia. There were other towns bearing the name of Antioch, one of which was further north, in Pisidia. Mark told himself that this mission was so important that the Lord seemed to be working extra hard to make it successful.

Before the return of the people of Antioch, Mark went to greet his cousin Barnabas. "*So, old mate, are you okay? Your leaving made me feel how important you are to me. Hope you don't blame me. Although I share a number of your remarks, I believe in letting time do its work. I hope to see you again soon in Antioch*".

"*I hope so too,*" Mark replied. "*Where is Paul? I will greet him*".

"*Hello brother,*" said Paul when Mark found him. "*Your departure was abrupt, and I did not understand the reasons that had made you abandon us. I hope all is well with you?*"

"*I'm fine, by the grace of God. I felt good to find my mother and the brothers I had left here.* I pray that your return trip to Antioch will be most enjoyable."

LONG TRIP

On the way back to Antioch, Barnabas and Paul, accompanied by Jude and Silas were joined by Rufus and Mona, his mother, and several others, among whom were Those who had come from Antioch. From towns to villages, from hotel to inn, the whole team organized themselves as best as they could to have a minimum of comfort. Fatigue could be seen on their faces and Mona, though still sad at the loss of her husband, managed to make sure everyone had had food to regain their strength.

At that time, the journeys were long, the roads difficult, and the temperatures capricious: too hot in summer, and too cold in winter. The springs and autumns were too short to be able to take full advantage of them. While a few made the trip on donkeys, many walked. But to make the trip between Jaffa and Antioch, there was nothing better than to use the seaway, when the navigation conditions allowed it.

Thus, the group of travelers first took the direction of Jaffa, making several stops, in particular so as not to tire too much the women who were accompanying them. Jaffa was considered by many to be the port of Jerusalem because it was the closest to the holy city. There were still other ports on the coast, but the remaining route would be too long and too tiring.

Mona was particularly worried about Paul. He hadn't taken time to rest since arriving in Jerusalem. Very busy, he did not spare his time to discuss with people and testify about what had happened to him on the road to Damascus. He also spent a lot of time with the apostles, asking many questions to deepen his knowledge of Jesus, his actions and his teachings. Paul got little sleep during this time, and he didn't take the time to eat well either, preferring to leave his share to the other brothers who were having a hard time. What Mona did not fail to notice, hence her concern for one who could have been her son, like Rufus.

"My child," she said to Paul, *"you look exhausted to me. You should eat a little and take it easy. These incessant journeys, the long vigils and the intensive study of the scrolls are a fatigue for the body, as the ecclesiast said. When crossing to Antioch, you should take the opportunity to rest, because certainly there is a lot of work waiting for you in Syria".*

Paul, touched by so much concern, replied, *"You must be right, Mother Mona. I don't realize that time flies. I get too easily carried away by my desire to speak to people, starting with those of my nation".*

"I'll ask the innkeeper to bring you a hot drink," Mona replied, *"and you'll get some sleep. It will be a long and arduous journey for all of us".*

"Jude, Silas and Titus must also need it".

Paul, addressing Rufus, asked with a smile, *"Is she like that with you too?"*

"So much so that she forgets to think of herself" replied Mona's son.

The next day, after two days of walking, Jaffa was in sight. The sea air was feeling good, and the group headed straight for the harbor in hopes of finding seats on a ship bound for Seleucia, not far from Antioch. Once on board, everyone took the opportunity to rest, hoping that the crossing will be done in good conditions.

RELIEF

*I*n Antioch, the arrival of the group of travelers returning from Jerusalem gathered many people. Believers from all over the region flocked to welcome Barnabas and his companions and listen to them recount how their journey went and above all, what the Apostles' response to their questions was.

At the invitation of Lucius, Barnabas addressed the brethren: *"As you know, we have made the long journey to Jerusalem to submit to the Apostles and the elders the questions you have given us. After consulting each other, they asked us to give you a letter that our brothers Jude and Silas here are going to read to you. Let's listen to them".*

Jude, after greeting the assembly and expressing his joy at being among the brethren opened the letter and read: *"The apostles, the elders, and the brethren, to the brethren of the Gentiles, who are in Antioch, in Syria, and in Cilicia, hello!*

Having learned that some men who had left our home, and to whom we had not given any orders, disturbed you with their speeches and shook your souls, we deemed it appropriate, after having gathered all together, to choose delegates and to send them to you with our beloved Barnabas and Paul, these men who laid down their lives for the name of our Lord Jesus Christ.

So we have sent Jude and Silas, who will tell you the same things with their mouths. For it seemed good to the Holy Spirit and to us not to place on you any other burden than what is necessary, namely, to abstain from meat sacrificed to idols, from blood, from strangled animals, and from fornication, things you will do well to beware of. Farewell".

Then, Silas spoke and added: *"Concerning other matters, the Apostles, the elders and the brothers of Jerusalem recommend that you follow the teachings which are given in the Synagogues. This will enlighten you on many points that would intrigue you".*

The Antioch brothers sighed with relief, and joy was on their faces. They commented among themselves on what they had just heard and thanked Barnabas, Paul, and all the others for coming out of the way to enlighten them on one of the issues that had created trouble and division.

In the evening, the travelers returning from Jerusalem met with Lucius who had a house large enough to accommodate several people.

Instinctively, Mona took matters into her own hands, aided by other, younger women. *"I thank the Lord for the kindness of this brother who welcomes us into his house to rest us there. I'll take care of you and cook you the right food. It has been a long and tiring journey, and we all need to regain our strength. Rufus and Titus will also give me a hand. Barnabas and Paul, you have a lot of work ahead of you with Jude and Silas. Regain your strength before you get back to it".*

Paul, touched by so much attention from this woman he had never known before, expressed his gratitude: *"Thank you, Mother Mona. You really are like a mother to me. I thank God for that. As for your son Rufus, he is a true chosen one of the Lord. You can be proud of him"*.

"Yes, I am," Mona replied. *"And Alexander too, his brother. I hope you will have the opportunity to meet him"*.

INCIDENT

few weeks later, in the Synagogue, many people gathered, in the midst of which were Barnabas, Saul, Jude, Silas, Lucius, Titus and Rufus. After reading a portion of the scriptures and singing the Psalms, Lucius addressed the congregation: *"We are delighted to welcome among us a brother who has just arrived from Jerusalem to visit us. This is Brother Cephas, one of the Lord's twelve apostles. Some of you know him as Simon Peter. It is a great honor for us to receive him and the brothers who accompany him, including our beloved Mark who is back among us."*

"Grace to you and peace in abundance through the true knowledge of God and of Jesus our Lord," said Peter. *"His divine power has given us all that makes it possible to live with piety, thanks to the true knowledge of the One who called us by the glory and the strength which belong to him. In this way we are granted the promised gifts, so precious and so great, so that, through them, you become participants of the divine nature, and that you escape the degradation produced in the world by covetousness".*

"It's a great joy to be among you. The brothers in Jerusalem have asked me to convey their greetings to you. I will stay with you for a while, and I will visit the surrounding areas."

The next day, when Mark had already found his bearings and his contacts with the people he knew, Jews and pagans, all urged him to invite the Lord's Apostle to share a meal with them to listen to him talk about the things of God. He addressed Peter: *"Several brothers want to meet you and hear you speak. It would be nice to accept their invitations."*

"I'll be happy to do it," replied Peter. *"Sharing the word of God is the main reason for my coming to the region. So I will go wherever doors open before me."*

Peter and Mark spent several days responding to invitations from the brothers. As soon as people heard that Peter was around, they all came to listen to him, so the houses filled up quickly, and many of them overflowed. Jews and pagans mingled and there seemed to be no particular problem around the table, as long as the food was taken with gratitude, thanksgiving, and simplicity of heart.

Sometimes at these meetings, Barnabas joined them. And with Peter, they ensured the teaching of the brothers, especially those among the Greeks who were converted and who needed to deepen their knowledge in the scriptures. It was not uncommon for Paul to join them as well.

One day, while Peter, Paul, and Barnabas were eating with pagans, Mark introduced himself and announced the arrival of brothers from Jerusalem, sent by James, the Lord's brother.

"Do we invite them to eat with us?"

Paul got up and went to meet them, while Peter and Barnabas left the table and left the house from behind so that the newcomers would not be scandalized when they see them sharing their meal with pagans. Because some Jews still did not accept to eat with the pagans. A few other people also followed them. But Paul caught up with them and angrily addressed Peter, *"Why are you running away from the brethren who have come from Jerusalem? If you who are a Jew live like the Gentiles, then why do you force them to Judaize by behaving like this? In addition, you took Barnabas and the others with you".*

Paul didn't mince his words. He still kept his impetuous character, stopping at nothing and no one, not even before the first of the Apostles. But Peter, keeping his calm, did not answer Paul's question. He would wait until things calm down before talking about it again.

That evening at home, Barnabas called out to Paul: *"Don't you think you were hard on Cephas? Some of the brothers were shocked at what they heard."*

"You know I always say what I mean," Paul replied. *"Even if it must cost me. I found his attitude inappropriate and told him so. We must not compromise on principles. I think he got my message".*

"Are you sure you yourself understood why he hid from the others, and why I followed him? Brothers, close to James, arrived from Jerusalem. You know how much they are attached to traditions, and how shocking them even to see Jews and pagans eating together. I think that Peter especially wanted to avoid a useless confrontation with them and to preserve the climate of fraternity which reigns here in Antioch between Jews and Gentiles. In any case, that's why I followed him, and not to cover up the fact that I fraternize with the gentiles. Are we not all brothers in Christ? Is there still a difference between Jews and not Jews, between slaves and not slaves? The brethren in

Jerusalem just need some time to understand this. And I think after that, everything will be fine."

"*Paul my child,*" Mona said, interrupting the discussion, "*you worry about a lot of things. Calm down now, and eat your meal in peace. Do not let yourself be overcome by anger. It's a bad counselor. But try to make peace with your brother. Both of you are precious to me.*"

The next day, in the middle of the morning, Mona looked for Barnabas busy with chores in the garden. The region of Antioch was green because it was rich in water. Grass growed fast, and what one plant in it made wonderful fruits and vegetables. Maintaining the gardens is therefore important, and Barnabas liked to take care of it whenever he found some time.

"*Joseph, we have heard from Epnaetus. He is in Rome and he invites us to join him there*".

"*Rome?*" Barnabas wondered."*So far? Do you plan to go?*"

"*It will bring us closer to Carthage,*" Mona replied. "*We will write to Alexander to tell him to come and join us in Rome. I miss him so much!*"

"*When are you planning to go?*" Barnabas asked.

"*Rufus says we have to let the winter pass because the seas are rough around this time. God willing, we will go next spring. I will announce it to the others*".

SEPARATION

As spring approached, Paul felt a little cramped in that region of Antioch. Ever since the incident with Peter, he had felt the disapproving gaze of the brothers, even though no one had told him anything about it. Because, knowing that he was close to Barnabas, no one dared to blame him openly, out of respect for the one who had introduced him into their community. And he himself did not see fit to explain it to them, still being convinced that he was right to do what he did.

Not having heard from the churches founded by him and Barnabas on their first missionary journey, he suggested to his former mentor to get back on the road and continue the work they had started: *"I think we stayed for too long in Antioch. I worry about what becomes of the communities we have established. Maybe they need help, encouragement, or even more teaching?"*.

"God is taking care of them, don't worry about them," said Barnabas. *"For me, I think especially of those who have not yet received the gospel in other regions. We must continue to proclaim the Good News where no one has heard of it yet"*.

Paul nodded. *"We will continue to speak to the nations. But in the meantime, let's revisit these communities* again".

"We will then have to inform the brothers and see if there are any among them who would like to accompany us. We will definitely need help. There's no shortage of work, "Barnabas suggested.

"You are right. I will ask a few others to come with us. I'm sure there will be many who will be happy to do it."

"There's Lucius, Jude, Silas, …" Barnabas began to suggest. But Paul interrupted him.

"Lucius has enough to do here. The Church of Antioch needs him. And Jude told me he was planning to go back to Jerusalem."

"So we have Silas and Mark left," Barnabas added.

Paul reacted forcefully. *"Mark? There is no question. We cannot take with us someone who had already abandoned us on our first trip. I still don't know why he did it anyway, but I can't count on him anymore."*

"Stop Paul," Barnabas replied. *"You are too intransigent! I know Mark. He is a good person, and he will be very useful to us again. And you know that in many things, he is irreplaceable".*

"If he abandoned us the first time around, he might start over," Paul added.

"Give him a second chance. You will not regret it. He proved himself with the brethren, and all of them bear good testimony of him. No one complained about him. We are the ones who need him, not the other way around".

"I don't want to take any risks". Paul's decision was made.

"Anyway for me," Barnabas replied, *"there is no question of giving him up. I will not leave without him".*

It was not only the family bond that led Barnabas to show solidarity with his cousin Mark. Not even their tribal bond of Levites. He knew Mark and had noticed his sense of practice. He was diligent in the Scriptures, and neither asked nor expected anything from others. He was quick to react to the most diverse situations, and even to anticipate events, taking the initiative to deal with any unmanageable unforeseen. Mark was practical. He did not care about protocols, but did not neglect any detail. That didn't stop him from paying attention to what was going on around him. He knew how to analyze situations and understand people. It also made him suspicious of those who wanted to take the top spots and show off. He was repelled by the vanity of things, and the least that can be said was that his Libyan origins had something to do with it. Nahum the prophet described the Libyans as *"helpers".* That is to say, assistants, supports or complements. And contrary to what it appears, being second was of great importance, because without him, whoever was considered first could not do much. Mark therefore took his role seriously, to enable those on the front line to fulfill their mission properly. And more than anyone, Barnabas was aware of it, knowing that he and Saul alone could not get far.

PATIENCE

A few days later, Barnabas and Mark got ready to take the boat to Cyprus. *"It's a pity the others don't come with us. There is a lot of work to be done in Cyprus,"* said Mark.

"Paul decided to go with Silas to visit the brothers in Syria and Cilicia, where we had been the first time. Luke is also on the trip". Barnabas replied.

"There are still plenty of villages in Cyprus that have certainly not yet received the Word," remarked Mark.

"Certainly," said Barnabas. *"We will go through them all and preach the grace of God. Then we will continue our journey to other areas where the Lord will lead us. Maybe in the north of Italy?"*

After a long moment of silence, Mark confided in his cousin. *"It's hard for me to understand Paul, I admit. He does whatever he wants, even if he takes the risk of frustrating others. As you know, I don't share his way of doing things. And he gets into trouble everywhere he goes. Not only that, but the people who accompany him also find themselves in difficult situations. I wouldn't be surprised if he ended up creating a vacuum around him, when he really needs to be surrounded, advised and helped".*

"Peter told me about his experience in Caesarea with Cornelius who was a pagan. At first he had resisted when the Lord told him to go and speak the Word at this centurion's house. Because he considered him unclean. But God showed him that he did not regard him as such. On the contrary, he told him, "What I have declared to be pure, it is not for you to declare unclean." So Peter entered Cornelius' house, announced the salvation of God to him and ate in his house with all his family. God does not exclude anyone. When he told his story in Jerusalem, some of our brethren reacted badly, accusing him of having eaten with the pagans. But when he explained to them what had happened to him, they calmed down. I think that was what he wanted to prevent from happening again when the brothers sent by James came to Antioch. But Paul did not understand it. And he reacted badly."

"Don't worry Mark," Barnabas replied. *"He will make his way and he will grow. The Lord is patient with all of us, and we, individually or together, will be transformed, purified and made fit to serve Him with more humility and efficiency. I think Paul will understand this pretty quickly, especially when he is accompanied by Silas who is, as you know, a prophet of God. That's why, even though I'm also disappointed with his behavior, I'm not more worried about it. He who saved him by bringing him into his kingdom will cause him to grow and mature, making him useful for the work of God."*

"But still," replied Mark, *"to attack Peter, the first of the Apostles, our big brother to all of us, it was daring. I felt like Paul, consciously or not, wanted to take his place from him by trying to take him back publicly."*

ROME

*I*n Rome, after a long crossing and a few stopovers, Rufus and his mother found Epnaetus. Rome is a big city. The capital of the empire. Mona, exhausted from the long trip, was still in awe of the world that swarmed there. *"I realize that our Cyrene is just a small town compared to this huge city."*

"Anyway," said Epnaetus, *"it's a great joy to see you again. I'll show you around the city, and meet the brethren here. Things are a little different from Antioch. The city is so big that several churches have sprung up here and there. I don't know if Priscilla and Aquila are in Rome now, but it would be nice to meet them. They were Paul's companions and worked a lot with him. They opened a church in their house. There are also Androchus, Junias and Herodion, who are parents of Paul. And there are people from all over the Empire. We find people from Greece, Egypt, Syria, Carthage, Spain, and of course also, Cyrene, not to mention those who come from Jerusalem and prosper here."*

"We went to a synagogue as soon as we arrived. It's impressive how many people of our region there were. They all spoke Punic among themselves,

and others also spoke Libyan. They all seemed to know you. They are the ones who told us where to find you," said Rufus.

Epnaetus replied: *"Despite the greatness of the city, all of the Lord's disciples know each other and know where each one lives. Moreover, without having done it on purpose, most believers live in the same part of the city, not far from each other: Aquila and Prisca, Andronicus and Junias, Urbain, Stachys, Apelles, Aristobulus, Herodion, Narcissus, Perside, Tryphene and Triphose and several others. Outside of the synagogues we frequent, we meet in each other's homes. By the way, this information must have gotten to Paul, since he wrote us a letter in which he mentions almost all of us. You will see, you will find so many of these people that you would think you were in the province of Africa, there are so many who are from there. Now that you are here, I will hurry to write to Alexander and inform him of your arrival. He can't wait to see you again. How are our brothers in Antioch?"*

BABYLON

*I*n Jerusalem, Mary was very happy to find her son Mark, back from a long trip. At home, he found Peter and several brothers who met regularly in this house. Strapola and Anna were also present. *"I have just returned from a long trip with Barnabas. I left him currently in northern Italy. The hand of the Lord is with him. He proclaims the Kingdom of God, and many miracles are performed by his hands".*

"I am glad my son." Is Paul with him too? Peter asked.

"Not at all. Paul returned to visit the churches he had founded with Barnabas. He is accompanied by Silas. Barnabas and I went to Cyprus first."

"In any case," replied Peter, *"your return is timely. I need your services, if that's okay with you. I have to go to Babylon, and I need your skills as an interpreter. Since your childhood, you have always liked to speak the languages of others. The Lord has endowed you with this talent. There will certainly also be Brother Silvanus with us."*

"Since my childhood in Cyrene, I have always lived among people speaking different languages", answered Mark: *"the Libyan, the Punic, the Hebrew in the Synagogue, the Greek, the Latin … Then in Jerusalem and in*

Galilee, I learned Aramaic. I'm sure people in Egypt understand Greek. In Alexandria there are many Greek and Latin speaking Jews. Yes, I will be happy to accompany you to Babylon".

Babylon was a small village located on the eastern bank of the Nile, just above the Delta. The Persians had built a fort there six hundred years earlier, then the Romans built another fort there on its ruins to control river traffic between upper and lower Egypt. The name Babylon derives from the history of rebellions in Babylonia in Mesopotamia. The prisoners, after a period of negotiations, were deported to this location which had since become a kind of place of refuge for prisoners. Babylon was therefore the gateway to the Delta and had become central to trade in Egypt, draining merchants from all sides. The strategic location of the city also made it a popular meeting place. This will be where the city of Fostat would be built, then, later, that of Old Cairo. The latter will be founded by the armies of the Kotama from the region of Saldae, now Bougie, and its neighbor Iguelgueli, which still bears the name of Jijel. Areas west of Carthage.

There was a synagogue in Babylon of Egypt attributed to Ben Ezra. Rabbis, scribes and doctors of the law kept many Torah manuscripts and various other documents there in a secret chamber called Gueniza. The rolls were placed in terracotta jars, then buried to prevent any deterioration. While he intended to address the Jewish community at the Ben Ezra synagogue, Peter also resolved to share the gospel with the other community, that of foreign refugees. Hence the need for Mark's skills in various languages.

Was Peter someone who saw the importance of this strategic city, or was it the Lord who instructed him to go there?

MONA

*I*n Rome, Epnaetus made Mona and Rufus visit the city, in the midst of crowds of people from all over. Mona was in awe of everything that was in the market and in the stalls. Goods from all over the world, wherever Pax Romana reigned, and even beyond. Persian rugs, linen, wool, cotton and hemp fabrics, clothes from Egypt, Mesopotamia and everywhere, spices from the East, Ethiopia, pottery, and objects of all kinds. There were even fruits she had never seen before, coming from the ends of the Empire.

Many of the merchants were only there for short stays. They would come to sell or trade their products, then move on to other regions to continue their trade, before returning on another season.

The streets near the Forum were full of mules and oxen pulling carts and chariots. There were also a large number of porters, the task of which was to load and unload the goods. This came both from the sea, but also from the paved roads of the Empire.

"Tell me Epnaetus," Mona asked, *"don't you miss Carthage?"*

"You are right, Mother Mona. Carthage is also a big city. It is as cosmopolitan as Rome. I can not wait to return to. I have family and friends there. In addition, there are many believers there who do not hesitate to cross the sea to come and share the gospel in Italy and in Europe. In Africa, I also went to Hippo, Cirta, Calama, and even to Lambesis. Alexander went to Caesarea of Mauretania, Tingis and Volubilis. It is a great land where the harvest is great. We must pray that the Lord of the harvest will send more workers".

"Don't forget the letter to Alexander then, my son," Mona reminded him.

"Don't worry, Mother Mona," Epnaetus reassured her. *"We are going to meet some travelers leaving for Carthage right away and I will give them the letter for Alexander. There is a constant back and forth between Carthage and Rome, and several people have offices in both cities. I am sure that in the next few weeks, Alexandre will receive the letter.* He travels a lot, and I don't know if he's in Carthage or on the move right now".

ARREST

*P*aul returned from his missionary trip with Silas, and hurried to Jerusalem before the holidays. It was important in his eyes to respect the divine appointments. Tradition had made them Jewish holidays. But in the scriptures they are called the Feasts of the Lord. These are the feasts of God himself, to which all men, Jewish or pagan, are invited. Although it is true that the Jews were the only ones to celebrate them. These celebrations therefore mainly brought Jews from all corners of the Empire and even beyond, allowing for encounters and reunions. Paul and Silas were delighted to rediscover the festive atmosphere of Jerusalem and to share special moments with their families and friends.

It was in the temple of Jerusalem that the Jews of Ephesus recognized Paul as he performed the rites of the celebration of this feast. In Ephesus where Paul had lived nearly three years, craftsmen grouped around a certain Demetrius had accused Paul of having undermined the worship of Artemis and other gods, by the preaching he made by announcing Jesus Christ as the Son of God. A riot ensued and Paul got away with it, while his companions had been badly beaten up.

In Jerusalem, the Ephesian Jews accused him of preaching against the Temple and against the Law of Moses. Paul was arrested and presented in Caesarea before the procurator of Judea, Antonius Felix to avoid a further riot. The latter already had a lot to do with the dissensions which divided the populations under his authority. Nero had declared that Caesarea was a Greek city, thus depriving the Jews of their right of citizenship, creating a segregation between Greeks, Romans, Jews and Samaritans. He soon hoped to be able to get rid of the prisoner who had been brought to trial. But he soon realized the Apostle's innocence. Fearing the reaction of the Jews if he were to release him, he decided to keep him in prison. Paul thus remained a prisoner for two years.

On the death of Felix, Porcius Festus was appointed procurator of Judea. He therefore decided to take over the business left unresolved by his predecessor. He summoned Paul to judge him: *"Paul of Tarsus. You were arrested because your accusers were complaining about your disturbing public order. You are a Roman citizen. Do you want to go up to Jerusalem, and be judged there over these things in my presence?"*

Paul presented his defense and, remembering what the Lord had told him two years before, he decided to appeal to Caesar. For indeed, after his arrest, he had had a vision in which Jesus said to him: *"Take heart; for as you bore witness about me in Jerusalem, so also must you bear witness in Rome"*. Paul then addressed Festus confidently: *"I will appear before the tribunal of Caesar, excellent Festus. This is where I am to be judged. I did no harm to the Jews, as you well know. If I have done any injustice, or some crime worthy of death, I do not refuse to die; but, if the things they accuse me of are wrong, no one has the right to hand me over to them. I appeal to Caesar"*.

Seeing the trial come to an end, the procurator concluded it with these words: *"You appealed to Caesar; you will go before Caesar"*.

PETRONILA

*I*n Rome, Rufus and his mother Mona moved into a small house on the immediate outskirts of the city. On the one hand, they were not isolated from other believers, on the other, they were far enough away from the hustle and bustle of the city. In their house, they often received people, especially those engaged in the preaching of the Gospel and who were passing through the capital of the empire. They thus found a place where they could stay, accomplish their mission, while benefiting from the necessary communion.

As they prepared to pray together, the brethren gathered that day at Rufus' home were surprised by the unexpected arrival of someone whom the Christians of Rome knew only by name. *"Beloved, allow me to introduce to you Mark, my childhood friend and my beloved in the Lord. He has been in the work with our beloved Cephas, Barnabas and Paul, in Jerusalem, Antioch and everywhere. He's coming from Jerusalem".*

People were both surprised by the visit of what was considered the second of the apostles, and delighted to see him in the flesh. *"Thanks Rufus,"* Mark began. *"And thank you to all of you for your welcome. I bring you greetings from the brothers of Judea and those from Antioch. These brethren are constantly praying for you and giving thanks to God for what they have heard about you. I am particularly happy to be with you. We arrived in Rome, my mother and I, several days ago. My father Aristobulus had a house here in Rome".*

Mona, sitting next to another younger woman, addressed Mark: *"Is Mary here in Rome? I can't wait to see her again. And I have a surprise for you, Mark".*

"Do you know Petronila? She's our sister in Christ, but she's also your sister, in a special way, I believe."

Mark, looking both surprised and delighted, addressed the young woman: *"So is that you? I am really happy to meet you. Our common father told me a lot about you and asked me to send you his warm greetings and to assure you of his permanent prayers. He also told me about your sister."*

Petronila, visibly moved, replied: *"I miss him. But I look forward to your presence. Let me introduce you to my sister Felicula. You have to come home. We certainly have a lot to tell each other. We will cook you a good meal. What would make you happy?*

Mona intervened in the discussion and said, *"He's like my children. They all like couscous".*

Everybody laughed. Couscous was a dish consumed in all regions of the Mediterranean. But in North Africa, it was the most popular dish. It was the feast dish. The one who accompanied families in all the events of life, from birth to death. It was considered the most complete, the most balanced dish of all. To the grains of wheat or barley, a sauce is added with vegetables of all kinds, depending on what was grown in each region, and mutton or beef, and sometimes both at the same time. It could also be prepared without the sauce and the meat, with whey or curdled milk. The composition could thus be varied ad infinitum. That's why people never got tired of it.

PRISONER

A short distance from Rome, on the Appian Way, soldiers marched at a steady pace, flanking a man - Paul - in his late fifties, carrying a piece of luggage slung over his shoulder. The path seemed long and the prisoner seemed to be dragging his feet. The Appian Way was also called the royal road, connecting Rome with many cities and provinces. It had been built three centuries earlier, and the authorities kept expanding it. A paved road, built by slaves and convicts, it was certainly the busiest road in Italy. A few decades earlier, a revolt of the slaves working on this route, led by a certain Spartacus, had broken out and Rome had severely put it down. Some six thousand crucifixions took place along the way, showing passers-by what it cost to revolt against Rome. Paul knew this story, but it was the first time he had pounded the pavement, a symbol of the Roman order.

While they were still walking, Paul and his companions were greeted by many brothers who heard the news of their arrival. All were happy with this surprise and regained courage after having suffered so much during the trip. The brothers decided to travel with them and accompany them to Rome.

Paul had remained in Malta during the winter months after the ship that transported him sank. As soon as better days arrived, the soldiers who accompanied him decided to hit the road towards the port of Puzols. Arrived at the port of this city permanently under the threat of Vesuvius, Paul has been authorized to spend a week with the Christians of the city, before resuming the road towards Rome, taking the Via Appia.

"Go on, have courage," said the decurion. *"If we walk as it should, tomorrow we will be in Rome".*

"Yes," Paul replied. *"God willing, it will be so that I find my freedom. I can't wait to appear before the Emperor. He would just have to hear what I'm going to tell him."*

Paul had never visited Rome before. He only knew the city from hearsay. Even though he knew it was tall, he still had no idea how tall and big it was. He was well acquainted with other cities of the Empire, such as Ephesus, Antioch or Thessaloniki, much larger than Jerusalem or Tarsus, his hometown. The people on the road to Rome were already far beyond what he was used to seeing even on market days. But Rome was a permanent market. The number of ships he had seen in the port of Puzols was already quite impressive. Ships from all over the Mediterranean, bringing all kinds of products back to their bunkers. Wine, olive oil, salt, wood, cereals, as well as wild animals intended for circus games… In Rome, you could find anything. On just needs to know how to look among the hundreds of stalls and shopping streets. There was also the cattle market, that of artisans and that of slaves.

The imperial city at that time had grown in a rather anarchic way, with poor districts, narrow streets creating a significant promiscuity, insalubrity, incessant noise, violence … the city had reached the record number of one million inhabitants.

One of the city's attractions was the Circus of Nero with its Egyptian obelisks. It was the place of the spectacle, with the bloody fights of gladiators, or condemned to ferocious beasts. To forget their misery, the people liked to be entertained by going to this place. It also happened that the Tiber overflowed and caused deadly floods, and even epidemics difficult to control. The authorities had not yet planned an urban plan and chaos constantly threatened these neighborhoods, which were often victims of fires, due to the burning of rubbish. The wind stoked the embers of poorly extinguished fires, and during the night, entire sections of these neighborhoods had to be evacuated to be able to fight the fire which broke out and which took quickly, being fed by the wood of the houses and the density houses stuck together. The beautiful imperial city was only in the affluent neighborhoods, while the daily reality of the population fell far short of the reputation of the city of Rome.

Rome prohibited the burial of the dead inside the city. All along the Appian Way visible tombs were built by families, rich or poor. Because for the Romans, the cult of the dead was important. This sometimes gave rise to competition between those who most wanted to honor their dead by building them increasingly sumptuous tombs. And they buried them as close to the road as possible so that people could see them and greet them. It was not uncommon to read an expression like *"Lollius Tullius Cicero to rest here near the path for passers-by to greet him"* engraved on a tomb. Paul was sad to see that the Romans had no other hope after death than to be greeted by passers-by. No one had explained to them the reality of the Kingdom of God and the hope that there was in Jesus for eternal life. God willing, he will be able to ensure that the Romans too can hear the gospel and be free from the worship of the dead.

"When you arrive in Rome, you will quickly have to find a place to stay. As a Roman citizen, you have the freedom to choose where you want to stay and complete freedom within your cottage. But you will not have the right to leave it until the day you are received by Caesar ", recalled the decurion. *"Until then, it might take a while. You have every interest in finding comfortable accommodation. Especially if you intend to have people in your home."*

COUSCOUS

*A*t the end of the week, Mark arrived at Petronila's house with Mary, his mother, Rufus and Mona. Epnaetus was already there, helping to prepare the table. In Carthage, Africa and Rome, people did not always have the same culinary traditions, nor the same way of eating. While the Romans liked to lie on their sides, leaning on their elbows, in Carthage and North Africa, people ate sitting on the floor, legs bent and crossed, around a low table, much like did people in Judea. Epnaetus, Rufus, and Mark, having traveled a lot, learned to adapt to all traditions. Which was not the case with Mona who always kept hers. Petronila and Felicula had therefore made sure that the spaces were wide enough for everyone to sit in the way that suited them.

It was the latter who greeted the guests, while her older sister was still busy in the kitchen. She was wearing a blue dress that reached her calves. The bandana she put on her black hair tied at the back highlighted the whiteness of her skin. Her older sister, on the other hand, had put on a long olive-green dress and a belt with orange patterns, while her head was covered with a floral scarf reminiscent of the colors of the belt. One cannot say that the two sisters did not know how to receive. The large room which welcomed them was simply furnished. Sofas, rugs, and three low tables put together to make one large, with pottery dishes and bowls resting on the long beige embroidered tablecloth all around, which covered the tables. There were also, in small plates, black olives and dried fruits.

"My sister and I are delighted to welcome those of our family and our loved ones, into the presence of the Lord," said Petronila. *"You are home. Put yourself at ease. We will soon be sharing our meal together."*

"Thank you for your warm welcome," said Mark. *"Your house is lovely, and even the neighborhood feels peaceful. What can I do to help you?"*

"Just prepare to tell us about the wonders that you have seen God operate around you, and give us news of our father Simon-Peter", replied Pétronille.

"You know girls," Mona interrupted, *"I knew Mark when he was a boy. He played with my children and often they ate together either at my house or at his mother's. They were like brothers. Inseparable. But because of disturbances in Cyrene, his parents decided to settle in Galilee and then in Judea. We missed them so much, until we found them again in Jerusalem long after."*

"Your couscous is delicious, my daughter," Mary declared to Petronila. *"So delicious that no one says a word, we are busy tasting it".*

The couscous semolina shone through the effect of the olive oil with which it had been coated, before being sprinkled with a sauce rich in various vegetables: tomatoes, carrots, turnips, zucchini, chickpeas … and above each of the dishes sat a large portion of meat. By the smell it gave off, one could tell it was lamb. In pitchers put on the table, there was water and wine, or more precisely, the fruit of the vine, as they used to say at the time. And it was Mona who broke the silence.

"All that's missing is Alexander in our midst to make my happiness complete. We're looking forward to his coming soon, God willing. Your couscous is delicious my daughter. You cook very well".

"Thank you, Mother Mona," replied Petronila. And Felicula added: *"She often prepares meals for the brothers and sisters passing through, or during the feasts that are organized. I learn a lot from her"*.

In any case, it makes me happy. Thank you for giving yourself so much trouble", Mark said. *"It is true that the presence of Alexander would have made this meeting even more wonderful. Is he still in Carthage?"*

"He moves a lot," Rufus replied. *"Sometimes he is in Carthage, sometimes in Cirta, in Calama, and even as far as the Pillars of Hercules. He goes where the Lord's service calls him"*.

Mark added: *"He's a bit like Simon-Peter then. Despite his age, he never stops traveling to share the Gospel or encourage the brethren. Before coming to Rome, I accompanied him to Babylon in Egypt. But previously he was in Antioch in Syria, and he also visited several cities in the region, not to mention the important work he does in Jerusalem. He's one of the pillars of the church there, and everyone is asking for him."*

Petronila was all ears. What did not escape Mark who continued: *"There is not a place that Peter has not visited. Besides, is that how, he told me, that you met Petronila?"*

"Indeed," replied Mark's new sister. *"He adopted me right away! He was constantly concerned about others and worried about our brothers. He*

spent a lot of time praying for them and urging them to take care of one another. What was remarkable was that he made no difference between Jews and non-Jews. He always said that there is only one God and that he should be made known to everyone, to the ends of the earth. His special relationship with the Lord gives him a strength that pushes him to always go further. I listened to him for hours telling the stories of Abraham, of the Sinai Covenant, of the life of the prophets, and explaining to us how, through all of this, came the person of Christ that God had promised to his people to save the world".

"Kind of like Paul, then?" Asked Epnaetus. *"Before leaving him in Antioch, he told me that he hoped to spread the gospel to the ends of the earth, so certainly in Spain."*

"This is indeed what he confirmed in the letter he sent to the brethren in Rome," Rufus added. *"He had said he hoped to stop here before continuing his journey to Spain. We haven't heard from him since. Hopefully he will be visiting us soon."*

Felicula, taking advantage of a moment of silence, began to sing spiritual songs. Her voice was incredibly soft. Even when the song was unfamiliar, she would lead the audience to follow her in melodies of great beauty. Petronila's sister memorized the songs she heard in study and prayer meetings, and herself wrote some that were taken up by the growing numbers of groups and churches in Rome.

The songs were generally inspired by the Psalms. For the poems of David were sung, as we read in the scriptures. Lyrical psalms, for wind or string instruments, … The sons of Korah as well as Asaph did not content themselves with following David in his compositions, but produced some of them themselves. They were so beautiful in the text and in the melody, they ended up appearing in the book of Psalms.

The new Christian communities, like the Jews, have fully integrated the songs into their meetings. It was also difficult at the beginning to distinguish a Jewish meeting from those of Christians, if it was not by the use of Hebrew and Aramaic by conservative Jews, those who were directly dependent on the doctors of the Law and the officials of the Temple, and those who, from the diaspora used their own languages, with a certain pre-domination of Latin, the language of the Empire. It was not uncommon for songs in different languages to be sung in the same meeting. And over time, some songs have been translated into various languages, allowing them to be sung in Latin, Greek, Persian, or whatever... At the same time, the new converts, coming from different countries, also brought their own musical styles. From Egyptian to Spanish, from Greek to Carthaginian, the variety of styles has considerably enriched the repertoires of Christian songs.

In these repertoires, one could find songs of praise and adoration, exhortations, laments, prayers, intercession, ... All were inspired by the Scriptures, essentially using the book of Psalms as a model.

After these long moments of sharing, Epnaetus ended the evening with prayer, while the rest of the group began to sing songs of praise and worship. As the guests prepared to return home, someone knocked on the door. Epnaetus opened the door and it was Amplias who had arrived.

"Good evening. I was told that you were all here, and I have come to inform you of the arrival of Brother Paul in chains to appear before Caesar".

"Paul in chains in Rome?" Mark wondered. *"But why?"*

146

"I don't know yet," Amplias replied. *"But he rented a house not far from here, and I learned he was free to have visitors."*

Mark sighed. Because being entitled to visits indicated that he was not under too great a strain. Besides, he wasn't thrown in the dungeon as one might expect. Because in the Roman prisons, the conditions of detention were very difficult. Many fell ill there, and even died from it before they even stood trial.

INTROSPECTION

*M*ark knew Paul well. The first time they met, his name was still Saul. It was in Jerusalem. And it was Barnabas who introduced him to the apostles. Peter had received him into his home for two weeks, and spoke to him about the things of the Lord, teaching him about how prophecies were fulfilled in Jesus, and the beginning of a new era in which the door of salvation was also open to the gentiles. Then he and Mark met again in Antioch where, with Barnabas, they had started a mission together to Cyprus and Asia. But along the way, there had been a dispute between them, and Mark had to interrupt the trip and return to Jerusalem. A few years later, preparing for a second missionary trip, Paul refused to embark Mark with him, causing his separation from Barnabas, who had mentored him for a dozen years. Mark still had these disappointments in his heart, and he still thought that Paul was too tough a character and that it was difficult to deal with him. But, that was not likely to prevent him from visiting him and inquiring about his situation, and if necessary, coming to his aid.

Early in the morning, therefore, Mark went to the address Amplias had given him. He knocked on the door and a soldier opened it for him. Still half asleep, he asked, "What is this?"

"My name is John-Mark from Jerusalem. Is Paul of Tarsus there?"

Praying in his room, Paul heard the voice of Mark whom he had recognized, while being surprised that he too was in Rome. He left his room, crossed the courtyard of the house, went to meet him and hugged him.

"Mark my brother! Paul exclaimed. *"What a surprise and what a joy to meet you in this place!"*

"I came as soon as I heard you were here," Mark replied. *"Don't worry, I will do everything necessary to make your stay as painless as possible. Will you tell me why you're in chains?"*

"There is a lot to tell Mark," said Paul. *"A lot of things have happened around me. But also, inside of me. Come on, let's go inside. We will be more comfortable. The long trip I have made since Caesarea has made me a little tired."*

Inside the house, the comfort was minimal, but sufficient. Paul enjoyed the status of a Roman citizen, and a semi-prisoner at the same time. Having yet to be tried, he enjoyed the privilege of being able to rent a house and enjoy some autonomy. The soldiers were only there to follow orders, knowing that their prisoner had no intention of running away. And as it was he himself who had asked to plead his case before Caesar, the guards did not seek to impose more on him, leaving him free to move, as long as it was happening inside the house that he had rented.

In the large room located in the center of the building, two sofas and a low table were arranged, offering the two companions the necessary amenities to chat quietly.

"The first time I met the Lord," Paul began, *"he asked me why I was persecuting him. And he added a sentence that I did not yet understood and which worked for me for a long time."*

"What was that? Mark asked.

"He said to me, it would be hard for you to kick against the goads."

"This expression is indeed not common," added Mark.

"I did not understand," continued Paul, *"that the Lord had taken me in hand, and that he had decided to work on me to free me from within. Free me from my pride, my prejudices, my pretensions… things that I did not see in myself. I believed I was doing things right and that God would be happy with me."*

"I don't know where you're going with this, but I'm following you, keep going."

"When I persecuted the early believers, I was sincere, I wanted to suppress those who I thought were dangerous to our faith. I thought I was standing up for our Faith and for the temple. I was deeply committed to this fight. What I did not know in fact was that my zeal exceeded this goal, and that behind all the efforts that I deployed, it was above all to show others that I was more zealous and more committed than them and that therefore, I would be more prominent and regarded by elders and priests. Without knowing it, it was my own glory that I was looking for."

"Ah! ", Said Mark".

"After my conversion, this character had not left me yet. I unwittingly continued to strive to outdo everyone else and rise above anyone else. Including in the church and including in my ministry and in my apostolate.

I was even a little irritated when I wasn't mentioned first when talking about the brothers. I couldn't stand being the last on the list. So I redoubled my efforts to be seen and recognized as better than others."

"But, what's wrong with wanting to be better than others, especially when you're doing good? "Mark asked.

"Competition is a great thing, when it's healthy. When it allows us to surpass ourselves and do even better. But not when it's at the expense of others. It is only good when it allows the group to move forward together without stepping on each other's toes. However, this is what I have done on several occasions. Without realizing, I took the place of others, I spoke when I should have let others do it and I stepped forward, relegating my brothers behind me, instead of giving them space to develop and flourish".

"I am impressed with your analysis and your awareness of your flaws," Mark replied. *"Defects that we all have, by the way."*

"Yes, you are right," added Paul. *"But it would seem that my evil was even deeper, and that the Lord had resolved to deliver me from it. And I didn't know how high the price was".*

"I don't understand, Paul. What are you referring to?".

"Wanting to be on the front lines, I was exposing myself, without realizing it, to all the dangers that lie in wait for those on the front lines in the fighting. I have known hard labor, beatings, imprisonment, and I have often been in danger of death. Five times I received the forty blows minus one from the Jews, three times I was whipped, once I was stoned, three times I was shipwrecked, I spent a day and a night in the sea. I have known hard work and hardship, I was exposed to many sleep deprivation, hunger and

thirst, many fasts, cold and destitution … It was like a thorn in my flesh which pursued me everywhere. I prayed to the Lord to deliver me, but he revealed to me that it was an angel of Satan who came to blow me up to keep me from being proud. It was the Lord himself who stuck it on me. And I had to accept to live only by grace. Sometimes I have wondered if, having the same name and coming from the same tribe, I was not like King Saul. Independent and stubborn, impatient and bossy."

"I know you have suffered a lot, Paul."

"Yes, but it was for that reason. Through all this suffering, the Lord was present. He never abandoned me. Quite the contrary, since he was teaching me to rely only on him, and no longer on my own strength, my intelligence or my wisdom, despite the excellence of the revelations he had made to me. As I explained to the brethren in Corinth, I was torn between struggles on the outside and fears on the inside".

"In the end, I can say that I was crucified with Christ. And if I live, it is no longer I who live, but Christ who lives in me. He wanted to develop his character in me and for me to learn to think and act like him. Because behind, he had plans for the Kingdom of God, and I was not fit to play any role in it without him preparing me for it. And that's what I'm trying to tell you my beloved Mark. I have learned. And as I learn, I evolve, I grow, I mature. I realize that you, Barnabas, Cephas and the others, have been put in my way to correct me and point me in the direction I should follow. But I wasn't always smart enough to figure it out. I only did my own thing. Which complicated my learning. I, the runt, the smallest of all the Apostles, if today I am in chains, it is because the Lord knows that on my own I would not have understood the mission he was entrusting to me. It was not until I was arrested in Jerusalem that he appeared to me in a vision to tell me that I should testify before Caesar. And this is the reason

for my presence here in Rome, and it is for this mission that he has been preparing me all these years. For who could have imagined for a single moment that a tentmaker from Tarsus would one day meet the ruler of the Empire?".

CARTHAGE

On the other side of the Mediterranean, there was also a large city whose civilization long rivaled that of Rome. Carthage was for centuries the most prosperous city in the region, long before Jerusalem, Alexandria or Rome bacame the cities they had become. The Carthaginians opened ports all along the shores of the Mediterranean and traded with all peoples. They had developed a war fleet so powerful that no one dared confront it. Until when Rome had developed and prospered. The two cities had become rivals and three bloody wars pitted them against each other, until the day when Rome, ally of the Numidians, gained the upper hand and destroyed the competing city.

Over time, she let her rebuild herself, while making sure she was no longer going to pose a threat to the Empire. Carthage regained its former glory and had become the most important city in Africa, under the control of Rome which ensured that it did not regain its military force which could made it a threat.

This was where Alexander was based, living there half of the year, spending the other half moving from town to town, from region to region, from plains to the mountains, announcing the Good News wherever he went and forming communities which he taught and trained before moving to new destinations.

While he was in his house in Carthage, there was a knock on the door. It was a maid who opened the door.

A woman, in her fifties, accompanied by two young boys, was there in front of the door:

"*Is this where Alexander lives?* "She asked in hesitant Latin.

All smiles, the servant asked in the same Latin, just as hesitant: "*Who should I announce?*"

"*My name is Photina,*" said the woman. "*I come from Samaria with my two sons*".

"*From Samaria? Come in,*" the servant invited them. "*Don't stay outside*".

The said maid just knew that Samaria was a distant land, without being able to exactly locate it. She didn't dare ask Photina for details.

Samaria was a territory located in ancient Israel that emerged from the Schism of the great Kingdom of Solomon. After his death, Israel split in two, Judah having taken its autonomy from the Northern Kingdom which had to choose a city not far from Shechem as its capital. This city called Samaria gave its name to the whole territory. And Shechem had been the place where Jacob had settled after leaving the home of his Uncle Laban, taking with him his wives, his children and all his possessions. For Jacob married his uncle's daughters and their maids, and had many children and acquired great wealth, despite the dishonesty of Laban and his sons. The Jews and the Samaritans knew well this story recorded in the book of Genesis. But not necessarily the other peoples who did not care about the internal histories of the people of Israel.

A tall man came forward and spoke to the woman in Aramaic. *"My name is Alexandre. Son of Simon. I am from Cyrene. Have I been told that you are from Samaria? What can I do for you?"*

"I am only a humble servant of the Lord," Photina replied. *"Yes, I am from Samaria and I came with my two children,"* she replied in Aramaic, happy to meet someone who spoke her language. *"I have heard of the grace that God has showered on Carthage, and I have come to the brothers to serve Him, if we can be of use my children and me."*

"Welcome in the midst of yours," said Alexander. *"Everyone here speaks Punic, Libyan and Latin. I hope you will adapt quickly to it. We will take care of you and make you comfortable. I must be away soon, but you will not want for anything in this humble abode. There is a lot to do and I am sure you will find your marks very quickly. The brothers will soon arrive, and you are going to tell us how you came to know the Lord?"*

ALEXANDER

*I*n Rome, Epnaetus had just received a letter from Alexander, informing him that he would soon be coming to meet his family. Epnaetus knew a lot of people in Rome. Particularly among those from Carthage. He was greatly appreciated for what he did for them and their families. Always ready, as in Carthage, to come to the aid of all those who needed it. His house in Rome was open to all who requested him, and all were in return, ready to render service to him when he needed it. This was the case for mail transport. Especially since these same people had also come to know the recipient of the letter entrusted to them, Alexander, son of Simon of Cyrene.

When He returned home, he informed Mona and her son Rufus. The mum was delighted and it could be seen on her face, which lit up. Mona's exterior often reflected what was inside of her. She did not hide her feelings or her emotions. Looking at her, you could easily guess what state she was in. When her face closed, almost this early, you could tell she was thinking of her missing husband or that she was worried about one of her children whom she had not heard from. But Mona was a courageous woman, who was quick to cast out bad thoughts, especially to take care of others and help them overcome their own sorrows.

As Rufus wondered if his brother had changed and what he might look like since he hadn't seen him in years, his mother spoke out loud. *"I'm sure he must have changed a bit,"* Mona said. *"He's definitely even stronger and more handsome. You too have changed Rufus. You are no longer the little child who played in the yard with John-Mark and the other children in Cyrene. I wish I had known when exactly your brother will be here. Because we would have to prepare for his coming. I would like to give him a real party to celebrate our reunion."*

Since their childhood, Simon of Cyrene had taught his children to always remain united and welded. They were not to let anything come and separate them. By teaching them the Ten Commandments, he also taught them the importance of respecting parents. *"For the Scriptures,"* he reminded them, *"promise long life to those who honored their father and mother"*. In fact, Simon and Mona never had to experience any rebellion from their children, even when in teenage years they began to show their desire for autonomy and emancipation. They were on good terms with the neighbors, and from childhood they played together and went to the same school teachers. Whether they were children of Greeks, Latins, Jews or Berbers, the children of Cyrene saw no difference between them, except in the contests and competitions which were organized to perfect their education. From time to time Cyrene had trouble with neighboring tribes. But children were still protected from adult conflict. Especially since sometimes it was resorted to violence. The parents of John, called Mark, were fed up with the attacks suffered during this disturbance, damaging their property and fearing for their own safety. As they were from the tribe of Levi, the father saw fit to approach Jerusalem, where his ancestors exercised their priesthood.

Simon and Mona were sad to see them go. And the children didn't quite understand why. They felt that the incidents were just passing events that fueled their imaginations as kids, even though they were growing up very quickly.

Alexander the eldest, had been given a number of tasks on Simon's estate early on. But the most important thing was to always watch over his brother Rufus, and in the absence of the daddy, also watch over his mum and the whole house. In fact, Alexandre had learned to take responsibility very early on.

RESPITE

everal months later, Paul still had not been received by the Emperor. But in the meantime, he was not wasting his time. He had been joined by Luke who was a doctor, and his house was open to the brothers to whom he brought advice and teachings.

"I am delighted that so many brothers are coming to visit you and that you have this freedom to receive them and to continue your work despite your chains," Mark told him.

In the city of Rome, Paul also had family who visited him: Andronicus and Junias who had known the Lord very early and who, by the quality of their work in the service of the Gospel, had won the respect of all, including the apostles. There was also Herodion who was discreet, but whose work was recognized by all.

"I admit that without you and Luke it would have been difficult for me to receive them all. I've been here for over a year now, and I'm still waiting to know the date of my trial."

"The Lord knows everything and he has the calendar in his hands," Mark replied. *"Nothing will be done outside of his divine plan"*.

Paul, the intrepid traveler, who had crossed almost half of the Empire, on foot, on horseback, on mule and by boat, now found himself inside a house, without having the right to go out. He missed walking and the sight of the mountains, the sea and the vast expanses of land was just a memory, though he still had hopes of resuming travel as soon as he was released.

What he loved most of all was going to cities where the gospel had not yet been announced. He loved to talk to people and share with them what was most important to him. He was not afraid of confrontation with the ideas of others, be they Jews or pagans. And he loved to see people convert and agree to be baptized in the name of the Lord Jesus.

Paul then spent time with the new converts, teaching them, educating them, and giving them recommendations for healthy living away from debauchery and drinking. After a while, knowing that he had to continue his journey, he encouraged the new churches thus formed to appoint leaders. Leaders who in turn were to teach others and help them grow. He recommended them to the grace of God and continued on his way to new destinations.

Paul's missions were tiring and exhausting. The roads were often dangerous and the assaults regular. This is why he was always accompanied when traveling to discourage malicious people.

Sometimes the danger did not come from the roads, but from within the cities themselves. For sometimes religious leaders, both Jews and Gentiles, were irritated by the Apostle's predictions. And not having found arguments capable of disassembling his rhetoric, they resort to violence. And Paul was scourged and stoned time and time again.

But in all of this, Paul only considered the benefits to people. He quickly forgot his pains and returned to work with the same zeal and the same commitment. In this, as in many things, he was an example to all who knew him or heard of him.

The time spent waiting for the trial, without knowing it, gave him a break. Rest for his body, so abused for all these years. A time of recovery and restoration. Because he was not done with his plans. He fully intended to continue his mission until the end of his life.

PHOTINA

In Carthage, in the house of Alexander, Photina is again surrounded by many people gathered to hear the story of her meeting with the Lord. News of her arrival quickly spread around Carthage, and many believers came to meet her. Some also brought with them unbelieving people hoping that the testimony of the Samaritan woman would encourage them to take the step towards faith. They finally had the opportunity to see a person who has physically met the Lord, except for Epnaetus. While Alexander was present in the Upper Room in Jerusalem during the outpouring of the Holy Spirit, he did not have the privilege of speaking personally with Jesus. Photina had a real discussion with the Messiah, and she told how it happened.

"I was in Samaria, and I went to draw water from our father Jacob's well in Sychar. There was a Jewish man sitting by the well there who asked me to give him a drink. I told him that Samaritans were not allowed to talk to Jews. I was hoping he would go away and draw my water quietly. But he answered me in an unexpected way. He told me that if I knew who was the person asking me for water, I would be the one to ask him. But he didn't even have anything to draw with. So I told him he was no better than our

father Jacob who had dug the well. I wanted to end our conversation, but he went on to say that anyone who drank this water would still be thirsty, but if someone drank the water that He offered to them, they will never be thirsty again for eternal life.. He said it would be living water."

Photina paused for a moment and drank a cup of water, then continued with her story.

So I told him to give me this water so that I wouldn't be thirsty and have to come back every day to draw it. Without answering me directly, in a few words he revealed all the secrets of my life. He told me who I was, who I dated, … Then I understood that he was a true prophet. I told him that we were all waiting for the Messiah, and he replied:

"I am, I who speak to you".

"So you have met the Lord in person?" Asked a young man present with the others.

"To tell the truth, it was he who had come to meet me. I didn't even know him, and I didn't even know he existed. Even though it's true, like everyone else, I knew a Messiah was coming someday. But he had come to the gates of my misery and transformed my life. His words to me entered my heart. Every word he used was in its place. And that touched me enormously. So I ran to the village and told everyone. His disciples joined him and all were invited to come to us, for he said that henceforth true worshipers no longer depend on a place, but on the spirit of truth. We can now worship God in Jerusalem, Samaria, Rome, Carthage and all over the world. He taught us, healed the sick, cast out demons, and worked great miracles among us. Through him salvation entered Samaria, while our traditions kept us locked in a narrow vision of the will of God".

MEETINGS

When Alexander landed at the port of Ostia, the sun was just beginning to rise. He came from Carthage and was on his way to Rome. Immediately after, he inquired about the route to take and took the Ostian Way, a paved road mostly taken by merchants with their loaded mounts, chariots and carts. He hoped to arrive in Rome before nightfall, to find his mother Mona and his brother Rufus. The address Epnaetus had given him was to help him very quickly locate them in this great city. This is why, arriving there in the middle of the afternoon, having walked for nearly eight hours, he went to a stall to ask for directions after indicating the address he was looking for.

At the end of a narrow street, he found a house, then knocked on the door. He was surprised to see that it was Rufus who opened the door for him. He didn't even have time to wonder how much his brother had changed.

"*Alexander*! Rufus cried out. The older one hugged the younger brother while laughing with joy. "*You are in good shape from what I see,"* added the eldest of Simon of Cyrene. *"So what about you,"* Rufus replied. "It's wonderful to see you again".

At the noise it made, Mona ran up. *"My son! My Alexandre!"*

Alexander took her in his arms and lifted her up.

"My son! I am so happy to see you again. Hope you have traveled well. Let me watch you. You missed me so much. Move in. I'll bring you some fresh water. You'll see, tonight I'm going to cook you a big dinner. Really, I missed you so much … I was afraid to join your father with the Lord, before seeing you again".

"Ah, mother! I have also missed you so much … Especially since Father left. But I knew you were in good hands, and I was waiting for the chance to come and find you. And this Rufus who is another part of me. I am so happy to see you both again. I should thank Epnaetus for all he has done to help us find each other. I hope he's okay. Where is he?"

"He'll be back soon, I think," Rufus replied. *He went out early this morning".*

"I hope he's okay? Everyone is waiting for him in Carthage", said Alexander. Then he added: *"You should tell me everything you've been doing in all this time. I look forward to hearing from you".*

"So what about you," Mona replied. *"It's up to you to tell us how you got around the world. You have traveled so much…"*

"Indeed, I went through the south, while you went through the north. Despite the sea that separated us, we finally find ourselves in the capital of the Empire".

In the meantime, Epnaetus arrived. *"I was told in the neighborhood that someone asked where my house was, and I immediately knew it was you,"* he told Alexander, hugging him. *"How are you fighting brother? I am so happy to see you again".*

"I'm fine, by the grace of God," Alexander replied. *"I see you haven't changed since we last saw each other. The Carthage brothers regularly ask for news from you. There are so many great things going on. I'll tell you about it later."*

Sitting on benches in the garden, the group spent the rest of the day chatting and sharing news. As each heard news from each other, they realized that the preaching of the gospel was received the same everywhere. The experiences of Antioch, Cyrene, Carthage, and Rome were quite comparable.

During the evening, Alexander began to tell his mother and others in the house how, since leaving Cyrene, he has traveled throughout the territories of North Africa. *"The territory is vast. It often takes several days of walking to get from one city to another. Fortunately, on the way, there are many towns and villages. Everywhere we went with the brothers who accompanied me, we were well received. People welcomed us into their homes, and we announced the Good News of the Kingdom of God to them. I was surprised how they received it, as if they had been waiting for it for a long time. We have seen changed lives, brothers and families who had not spoken to each other for a long time, reconcile and come together to celebrate the Lord in each other's homes. The sick were healed, and joy could finally be seen on the faces of the people. Sometimes our hosts wanted to keep us with them, but we explained to them that we had to continue on our way to proclaim the Kingdom of God. So we spent time training them, consolidating the groups, then helping them to designate leaders capable of taking over after our departure. We were even surprised, when we arrived in some places, to see that people were waiting for us after learning what had happened in the other places we had visited. What helped us the most was when there were synagogues, because it made our work easier. Because in general, people already know the scriptures and are waiting for the coming of the Messiah. When they were told that this Messiah was Jesus of Nazareth, many rejoiced, because they had already heard about Him through the testimony of pilgrims who had visited Jerusalem, but without knowing the details. It was enough then to take the scrolls of the Law as well as the books of the Psalms and the Prophets to show them that Jesus is the Messiah announced by the Scriptures. Many became believers and were baptized.* Again, once hope had returned, communities would come together to deepen their knowledge of the Scriptures, and disciples would rise up to share the Gospel in the surrounding areas. One of the places where we worked the most was Tripolitania. In Oea, Leptis and Sabratha, live people from all horizons. There are Greeks, Romans, and indigenous. Among them there were also many Jews. After their conversion and baptism, they helped us proclaim the Gospel to other communities. Really they are doing a great job. One does not feel animosity towards them, and relations are peaceful, allowing the Word of God to be proclaimed more promptly. After our departure, to continue our journey, we always left communities organized around a council of elders, with teachers able to faithfully transmit the teaching of the Apostles."

"And how did it go in Carthage then? Rufus asked.

"Before we got to Carthage," Alexander replied, *"we passed through other towns. For that, we sometimes had to make long detours to get there. After the assassination of King Ptolemy, there was a revolt all over the land. Two Berber leaders rose up against Rome, and there was a revolt that lasted four*

years. We had to stop for a while, so as not to get involved in the fighting. Aedemon and Sabalus had recruited large troops, and violence reigned for some time. We stopped in the Aures Mounts, then in the big cities of Cirta and Hippo, or smaller ones like Calama and Taghaste or even Madaura. In this city where a university was built, people were curious to discover our faith, and the debates were numerous and fruitful. Everywhere the reception of the word of God has been magnificent. We can no longer count the number of baptisms there were there. In addition, the people seemed to already have a knowledge of the Scriptures, and the travelers reported the news that a man had come to Jerusalem and declared that he was the Messiah, doing all kinds of miracles and wonders. It was enough to give them the details and explain to them that this Messiah is Jesus of Nazareth for the people to adhere completely to the new faith".

Pausing, Alexander looked at his mother who was busy making a hot drink.

"Mother, rest a little, and stay with us. You worked a lot today".

Thereupon Rufus interjected, saying that she was always like that and that she never stopped. *"She can't rest,"* he complained to his older brother.

"I am coming, my children. I'm coming very soon. You have to tell us how you got to Carthage".

"In Carthage, we didn't do much. In Cirta, we learned that there was already an established community in Carthage. When we got there, we were able to confirm it, not knowing that Epnaetus was already established there. Therefore, I will gladly let him speak to tell you about it. I'd rather tell you what I did after I left Carthage. Because we had formed teams of evangelists to go crisscross Africa and Mauretania, visit the tribes of

Numidians, Musulams, Getulas, and the most remote cities and villages to announce the Good News of the Kingdom of God, such as the Lord had commanded us. We crossed the port of Iguelgueli to arrive at the region of Saldae and Tubusuptu. Facing Saldae, there are mountains called the Babors. No one could have suspected the way the gospel was received there. It was like wildfire. It was enough to show up at the gates of villages and towns for crowds to gather and declare their faith in the Lord Jesus. We have seen repentance and reconciliation between villages that have been at war with each other for decades. The elders of the villages made their houses available and several groups were formed in these innumerable localities. In winter, it snows a lot, and believers gathered together in whole families. So we built basilicas, sometimes up to three per village. There, we don't speak Greek, Latin, or even Punic. Only the Libyan. Knowledge of my mother tongue, adapted for the occasion to speak local, was very useful to me. I was very moved by the warm welcome from these people. Then, in the spring, we continued to the western plains, passing through towns like Icosium and Caesarea. The latter was the capital of the Kingdom of Mauretania, before Rome annexed it. The people are literate there and the debates in the public places were very numerous. Peaceful, but very sustained. There were among the inhabitants philosophers, grammarians, physicians, ... and the debates did not cease until they saw the miracles and wonders which were performed by the Lord in their midst. For there are many high places and occult practices in the region, But nothing could resist the power of God. New converts told me that they intended to go to Volubilis, the king's second home, via Siga and Tingis and the Pillars of Hercules, and proclaim the gospel along the way. That's why I didn't go further, and I returned to Carthage to join our brother Epnaetus. But before that, the brothers told me that a former Roman officer native to the region of Lucu, son of a Berber pig farmer, and himself versed in philosophy, had traveled to Judea and would have met the Lord himself. On returning to the country, Dernatinus, that was his name, had begun to announce the Good News. The brothers would then have helped him by explaining more exactly the Scriptures to him.

"Did you know that Paul is a prisoner in Rome? "Rufus asked. *"He was taken from Caesarea to be tried by the Emperor himself. If you want, tomorrow we will visit him. There is John-Mark who takes care of him. We will pick him up from his house, and we will go to the residence where Paul is. He is free to receive whoever he wants".*

"I didn't know Paul personally. But I've heard a lot about him. I can't wait to meet him. And this dear John-Mark. How happy I will be to see him again…"

Mona, not missing any of what was being said, took the opportunity to fly: *"I will cook them a good meal that we will take with us."*

VISIT

*T*he next day in the middle of the day, Mona said that she was ready, with Mary, to go and bring the meal to Paul and his possible companions. She had got up early in the morning to be on time to visit the prisoner. Epnaetus preceded the group to John-Mark's to retain them while awaiting the arrival of Mona and her two sons.

"You know, I met Paul when he was still called Saul", said Rufus to his brother. *"He had come to Jerusalem with Joseph. People were afraid of him, because before his meeting with the Lord, he had persecuted a lot the believers. Today he has totally changed, and it is religious leaders who persecute him for his faith in Jesus Christ. They should be there on the day of the trial, when Paul appears before Caesar. Because they will have to explain the basis of their accusations. But Paul remained firm, and took advantage of his stay in Rome to make himself useful for the brothers and sisters of the whole region. Mark was already there when Paul was brought in by the soldiers. But the latter had no problem with them, having had time to know him from Caesarea. They trusted him, and did not prevent him from receiving his friends".*

Mark was at the door of his house, waiting for Alexander to arrive. His face was lit by a broad smile lit by the morning sun, when at last he saw him arriving with his mother and Rufus.

"I no longer know if you are still the son of Cyrene, or have you become Alexander of Carthage, or even if you intend to become Alexander of Rome," John-Mark said jokingly. *"I am so happy to see you again. Not as much as your mother, but still".*

*"You remind me of when you were children in Cyrene. The only thing missing is Simon who is with the Lord now,"*said Mona.

"We will all join them sooner or later," said Mary. *"Me"*, added Alexandre, *"I am happy to find John, this dear Mark and Mother Mary"*. Then, turning to his friend, he added, *"I've thought about you a lot, you know. When I was telling how I came to know the Lord, I often used your name to explain the role you played in our conversion to Rufus and to me."*

"Would you like to come in to my house and have some water before you go to visit Paul?""

"Another time, my son," Mona replied. *"We have to go quickly while the meal is still hot. And not to tire the arms of Rufus who carries the basket. Moreover, we must not leave poor Paul alone".*

"Don't worry Mother Mona, he's far from alone. He was joined by several brothers, such as Luke, Aristarchus, Onesimus, and others. That's why I take the liberty of taking my leave from time to time. Besides, I will soon be going back to Jerusalem myself".

Paul was surprised to see John-Mark and his mother arrive, accompanied by Mona, Rufus and Epnaetus, as well as a stranger.

The greetings were warm. Paul didn't seem to be complaining about his condition and the group were happy to see that he was in great shape.

It was Mona who introduced her son. *"I am delighted to introduce you to my eldest son, Alexandre who has just arrived from Carthage. I had already spoken to you about him several times".*

The two men looked at each other as if to better discover each other. *"So you are Rufus's brother? He and your mom told me so much about you. It's a joy to finally be able to meet you. Your mother is very lucky to have you. I consider her myself to be my own mother. She is a blessing for all who approach her".*

"I am aware of the grace given to me by the Lord in having parents like this. You would also have loved our Father Simon. I'm sure you know his story a bit. He had the privilege of accompanying the Lord to Golgotha".

"Come in," Paul invited them. *"The other brothers went out for a while. I think they'll be back soon. I am sure you will have a lot to tell us. I can't wait to learn more about what the Lord is doing in Carthage. I do not know this city about which it is said so much good. And the Carthaginians seem to compete in zeal for spreading the Gospel. Mother Mary, I didn't expect to see you again anytime soon. I'm so happy about it. I knew you were in Rome, but I didn't expect to meet you there. I hope you will give me news of the brothers and sisters in Jerusalem."*

APPEARANCE

A few weeks later, the Roman officer in charge of Paul's custody informed him that Caesar had consented to receive him in order to listen to him. Almost two years after his arrest, his incarceration began in Jerusalem and then in Caesarea. He traveled in autumn and winter by boat to Rome. The weather conditions made his trip extremely difficult, resulting in a shipwreck in Malta. His Roman period allowed him to meet many Christians in Rome and to teach them. Likewise, he took the opportunity to write to the churches he had founded in Asia, to give them news of him and to give them words of encouragement. That same churches have shown that they have not forgotten him, and Paul has received generous donations from them, enabling him to support himself in the capital of the Empire. On the contrary, the period of imprisonment, which was supposed to be a period of immobilization, was rich and dynamic. On the eve of his appearance before Caesar, Paul took stock of his stay under the chains, and raised his hands to heaven to thank his God and pray for the Emperor.

"You know Paul," the decurion told him, *"It will all depend on his mood. He can release you just as he can condemn you, without having to justify*

himself. You do not know of any senator here who can intercede with him on your behalf, and it is difficult to influence his decision. We here know who you are, and we are even convinced of your innocence. But we can't tell the Emperor. Moreover, everything will depend on what your accusers who will come from Jerusalem say, and how they present their accusations against you".

"Thank you, decurion," Paul replied. *"I don't worry about it. I have heard them accuse me before in Jerusalem and Caesarea. They couldn't provide any proof of what they were saying. Moreover, they always act the same way. I have already been told how they also accused Jesus of Nazareth before me, before Pilate, the Governor of Judea. Their accusations were so rambling that Pilate ended up saying that he did not find him guilty of any of the accusations made against him. In addition, I have a God who is alive and who will stand by my side on the day of the trial. I have so much to say to the Emperor. I just hope he gives me the time I need to do it. Caesar, you and every man need to hear the message that I carry with me, that there is a Savior, and he invites you to believe in him to become new creatures. This is what I did, and this is what any man who cares about his salvation should do."*

RELEASE

On the date set by the Emperor, Paul's accusers did not come forward. The religious authorities in Jerusalem did not send anyone to Rome to present their grievances against Paul, and Caesar was astonished. *"Where are your accusers?"* Nero asked. *"Do you know what you're being accused of, and what do you have to say in your defense?"*.

Paul, standing in front of the emperor, began by greeting the one who was to judge him. *"I am honored to be in front of you Caesar. If my accusers had found anything to present against me in front of you, they would not have failed to come forward to confirm their accusations. But as you can see, having no argument to develop, they did not have the courage to come before you. Know oh Caesar, that I am a Roman citizen born in Tarsus, in Cilicia. I am a Jew from the tribe of Benjamin, and I faithfully serve my God and strive to be of service to my neighbor always. I travel the countries announcing that wherever men are found, God extends his grace towards them, wanting only their salvation and their good. It was for this salvation that he sent his son Jesus of Nazareth, who was a good man, who went from place to place to proclaim the Good News of salvation. According to this Good News, all men must repent and turn away from evil to do good, worshiping the God who is in heaven. It is because of this preaching that I am in chains before you, O noble Caesar".*

"I have not been told that you bore arms against the Empire, nor that you have an army behind you. How are you a threat to the citizens of Rome? Asked Caesar.

"Our weapons are spiritual, Noble Caesar," replied Paul. *"They are powerful for doing good, not evil. To help the poor, support widows and orphans and heal broken hearts. Our God called us to bless and not to curse. And his kingdom is not of this world. He is enthroned in the heavens, and the earth is but his footstool."*

At these words, Nero was surprised. *"Why have I been taken this man? I don't see anything wrong with what he says. If he has beliefs different from those of his accusers, that does not make him a criminal. Let us stop bothering him, then, and let him be released immediately."*

It was joy in Rome. All the Christians in the city joined Paul in greeting him before he left. The latter could no longer remain inactive, and he decided to return to Colossi to join Philemon who had not abandoned him during his two years of captivity and who had even contributed to the expenses of the apostle during his stay in Rome.

So many of them accompanied him on the Ostian Way to greet him once again, in the hope of seeing him again soon. There was Amplias and Apelles, who, despite the hardships he was going through, had made a point of greeting Paul before his departure. Along with Alexander and Rufus and their mother, there were also Patrobas, Hermas and Phlegon. They were joined by Prisca and Acquilas, Mary and Andronicus, followed by Urban and Herodion as well as many other disciples saddened by the news of Paul's departure, after rejoicing at his release.

At the end of the whole day's journey, arrived at the port of Ostia, Paul knelt on the ground, imitated by all his companions and pronounced a prayer which he made ascend to heaven. When he had finished, he looked at his loved ones and said to them, raising his hands to heaven: *"The Lord bless you and keep you. May he make his face shine on you and grant you his grace. May the Lord turn his face to you and give you peace"*. Then, getting up, and seeing the weeping faces, he gave them a big smile and said, *"It's time to go. If I stay longer, I will also start to cry"*.

Paul boarded a ship with Luke heading for Colossi where Philemon had already prepared accommodation for them, as he had requested by mail during his captivity. The other companions each left to their occupations, leaving the brothers in Rome to continue their spiritual life enriched by the teachings that Paul had been able to lavish on them during his stay in the city.

Epnaetus had already returned to Carthage, while Alexander had stayed longer in Rome, having spent sufficient time with Paul to get to know him better. The two men appreciated each other very much, and a few weeks after Paul left for the province of Asia, Alexander returned to that of Africa, vowing to keep in touch for other projects in the Lord.

Rufus, meanwhile, remained in Rome with his mother, serving the local community made up of many churches. Mark went back with his mother to Jerusalem, and joined Peter and several brothers and sisters who always met in their house.

REPRISE

*I*n Carthage, Epnaetus was busy with brothers and sisters from all over the region. The economic dynamism of the city meant that people traveled a lot. Both northward by sea, but also inland. Thugga, Sicca Veneria, Taghaste, Hippone, and even up to Cirta and Auzia. It also favored exchanges between believers in different towns and cities. Of course, Carthage is the most important of all the cities of Africa and Epnaetus received at his home all the believers who stayed in this city. He always found a way to accommodate people, even if sometimes he called on other brothers to receive the surplus visitors, especially during the holidays.

Over the past few weeks, more and more Jews have arrived from Judea, fleeing the looming atmosphere of war. Religious leaders took it into their heads to liberate the Land of Israel from its Roman occupant. At the beginning, the revolts were sporadic, and the Roman soldiers present on the spot were quick to subdue them. But in recent months, the revolts had picked up and so had the repression. The unrest in recent weeks had prompted several families to leave their land and property to find refuge on more lenient land. Epnaetus organized to welcome those of the brothers who knocked on his door, and solidarity organized to provide shelter for the refugees.

At Epnaetus, there were three times of prayer a day. The Terce around nine in the morning, the Sext around noon and None around three in the afternoon. At each of these times of prayer, Epnaetus favored reading a portion of the Scriptures simultaneously translated into the Punic and Libyan languages. Because not all spoke Greek, even if at that time, the majority of residents of large cities spoke Latin. But there were people who came from remote areas, where only Punic or Libyan was used. Those who attended synagogues also knew a little Hebrew, from weekly liturgical readings. It was, however, the Septuagint, the Greek version of the Scriptures, which had been translated from Hebrew in Alexandria three centuries earlier, that was prevalent. Some people wondered why we would not think of a Latin translation of the Scriptures, especially since Carthage was full of skills[1].

After several weeks of absence, Alexandre was back in Carthage. His stay in Rome was very fruitful, and his meeting with Paul, very enriching. They even considered plans for the future together.

"So was your stay in Rome beneficial?" Epnaetus asked Alexander. *"I'm glad you are finally back, because there is a lot of work here, and I really need help."*

"I was very happy to see my mother again. Despite her age, and the fact that she lost her husband, she remained very dynamic. It must also be said that

---

[1] That would be done two centuries later, in the time of St. Cyprian, bishop of Carthage where the Vetus Afer was produced as the first latin Bible translation.

Rufus takes good care of her. I had the joy of meeting the apostle Paul and witnessing his release after his trial before the Emperor. He was acquitted, after Nero heard him plead his case. He testified of the Lord before Caesar. We were all fortified by this victory, and it makes us want to move forward even more. He had been wrongfully accused, but he was released because no one could prove his guilt."

"You should have brought him back with you," said Epnaetus. *"First to make him discover Carthage, then to teach us and help us better understand the depths of the word of God. The brothers here would have been delighted to meet him. I got to know him very soon after his conversion, and we got along very well".*

"Don't worry Epnaetus. Carthage already carries within it the seeds of great doctors who will shine throughout the world. Paul told us he wanted to do one last tour of Asia before coming back to Rome. He asked Rufus and me to accompany him to Spain to speak the word of God there. It will be an honor for me. It's about the same distance from Rome or from Carthage. Plus, you can walk through the Pillars of Hercules in just a few hours. Brothers from Tingis will be able to strengthen the churches there, once established. As for Mark, he returned to Jerusalem. He needed to accompany his mother who is being aging now. She might need him by her side."

PROJECT

Many thousand miles away, in Antioch, the brothers still had not heard from Paul and his trial. Prayers for him had not ceased, and the church was always on the lookout for information from travelers to bring back. Perhaps this would explain why some church leaders felt the need to teach the faithful about the persecution. Lucius recalled the words of Jesus reported by John- Mark. *"Take heed to yourselves. You will be delivered up to the courts, and you will be beaten with rods in the synagogues; you will appear before governors and before kings, for my sake, to serve as their testimony"*. Wasn't that what had happened to Paul? and to many others too. Lucius continues: *"Our brother Luke, the beloved physician who is with Paul, also related to us these words of the Lord:"When you are brought before the synagogues, the magistrates and the authorities, do not worry about how you will defend yourself neither about what you say". I am sure he reminded our brother Paul of them to strengthen him. And I have no doubt that the Lord will do it and that soon we will see them again among us"*.

A few weeks later, it was Mark who had arrived from Jerusalem. He was the bearer of good news.

"Have you been informed of the release of our brother Paul? He may be currently in Colossi, and he is preparing to tour Asia again. After that, he plans to go to Spain. I was happy to witness his release. Perhaps he will come to Antioch once again? I know he asked Alexander and Rufus to accompany him to Iberia. I intend to go to Ephesus to find Timothy. I might be of assistance to the Lord's work in this area".

In Paul's plans, the end of his mission in this land was to take place in Spain. Because at the time, it was believed that Spain was the end of the earth, and that there was nothing beyond the ocean. The Greeks also called the land of the Moors, located just south of Spain, the Land of the Hesperides, Hesperos. That is to say, the land of the West. This is where the sun was setting, and therefore, there could be nothing beyond. The very name of Hispania is also a direct descendant of that of Hesperos.

Spain was also something else in the Spirit of Paul. It was the most Latinized country in the entire Roman Empire. The Spaniards were open-minded and their character was quite different from that of the Greeks. Spain saw only brief episodes of war and suffered less than the eastern parts of the Empire, although its capture by the Romans was not easy. The Punic wars between Rome and Carthage had greatly affected the coastal cities, but the populations had taken refuge inland, and it was not until Carthage was defeated in the third punic war that the Roman legions penetrated until north of the Peninsula. And it has seen many epidemics and famines, with periods of drought making farming more difficult. Its proximity to the countries of Mauretania Tingitana and Caesarea as well as that of Gaul, has enabled it to overcome the successive crises experienced by the populations. And Spain was known for its resilience in the face of calamities. Once the crisis was over, the Iberians resumed work to repair the damage suffered, and quickly regained the upper hand. Agriculture was developing very quickly in this country alongside breeding and fishing.

Moreover, the Phoenicians had also opened many counters on the Spanish and Catalan coasts, like that of Cartagena, Spanish replica of the name of Carthage. There were still other cities renowned for the quality of their products, such as Cadiz, Malaka and Tarraco.

Paul knew that the Hispanic mission could be long. But on the strength of his experience, and assisted by the two brothers from Cyrene, he intended to act quickly by forming numerous groups which would themselves take charge of evangelizing the rest of the Peninsula. Christians from Carthage and Mauretania would come to help the new converts to develop the newly established churches.

SPAIN

*I*n Cadiz, where Paul, Alexander and Rufus, as well as a few companions disembarked, the priority was to find the synagogue in order to get there on the following Sabbath. *"In the meantime,"* said Paul, *"let's explore the country. Everyone here speaks Latin. If my Greek is not understood and my Latin is insufficient, I will count on you to act as my interpreters."* "By going as far as Cadiz located in the west of the Peninsula, Paul and his companions intended to return to Catalonia by evangelizing on the way.

"Don't worry Paul," said Alexander. *"When we talk from the heart, everyone understands. And when they see the power of God, the words won't matter much. In Carthage, we all spoke Latin. But many preferred Punic or Libyan. But in any case, the message penetrated hearts and transformed lives. That is what matters".*

The following Sabbath, Paul and his companions went to the synagogue. A Jewish community had settled in the city for decades and traded with Judea, exporting the best products from Spain. Everyone made them feel welcome, recognizing that they were not from the region. After the reading of the law and the prophets, the leaders of the synagogue said to them: *"Men and brethren, if you have any exhortation to address to the people, speak up".*

Paul stood up and said: *"Men of Israel, and you who fear God, listen! The God of Israel chose our fathers and honored this people during their stay in the land of Egypt, before coming out with his mighty arm. He fed them for forty years in the wilderness and brought them into the land of Canaan after destroying seven nations. He gave them this land, flowing with milk and honey, as their property. After that he gave them judges, until the prophet Samuel. They then asked for a king who could rule over them. And God gave them Saul of the tribe of Benjamin. Then, having rejected him for disobedience to the divine word, he raised up for them David as king, to whom he bore this testimony: I have found David, a man according to my heart, who will do all my wills. It is from the seed of David that God, according to his promise, raised up to Israel a Savior, who is Jesus. Moses said: The Lord your God will raise up for you a prophet like me from among your brethren; you will listen to him in whatever he says to you, and whoever does not listen to this prophet will be cut off from among the people. All the prophets who have spoken successively since Samuel also announced those days. Before his coming, John had preached the baptism of repentance to all the people of Israel".*

Then, after a moment of silence where he looked at the crowd to make sure that they were following his speech, he added: *"Men and brothers, sons of the race of Abraham, and you who fear God, it is to you that this word of salvation has been sent. For the inhabitants of Jerusalem and their rulers disregarded Jesus, and by condemning him they fulfilled the words of the prophets which are read every Sabbath. Although they found nothing in him that was worthy of death, they asked Pilate to put him to death. And, after they had fulfilled all that was written about him, they took him down from the cross and laid him in a sepulcher. God thus fulfilled what he had announced in advance by the mouths of all his prophets, that his Christ was to suffer. But He raised him from the dead. He appeared for many days to those who had gone up with him from Galilee to Jerusalem, and who are now his witnesses to the people. And we, we announce to you this good news that the promise made to our fathers, God fulfilled it for us His children, by resuscitating Jesus, according to what is written in the second Psalm: You are my Son, I have you spawned today. That he raised him from the dead, so that he will not return to corruption. This is what he said, saying: I will give you The holy graces promised to David, those graces which are assured. This is why he also says elsewhere: You will not allow your Saint to see corruption. Now David, after serving the purpose of God in his time, died, was reunited with his fathers, and saw corruption. But he whom God raised up did not see the corruption. You are the sons of the prophets and of the covenant that God made with our fathers, saying to Abraham: All the families of the earth will be blessed in your seed".*

Finally, he ended his speech with these words: *"To you first God, having raised up his servant, sent him to bless you, turning each one of you from his iniquities. Know therefore, brothers and sisters, that it is through him that the forgiveness of sins is proclaimed to you, and that everyone who believes is justified by him from all things from which you could not be justified by the law of Moses. So beware that what is said in the prophets does not happen to you: See, contemptors, be astonished and perish; because I am going to do a work in your days, a work that you would not believe if it were told to you".*

Those who were present in the synagogue were greatly moved. The rabbi took the floor and confirmed that some witnesses who returned from Jerusalem had indeed affirmed that a man had been crucified despite the fact that he had only done good and that nothing was found in him that could condemn him. *"We will listen to you again next time,"* he said. *"And will be happy to welcome you. We want to know more. But tell us, what must we do to be saved then?"*

Paul replied, *"Repent of your sins and be baptized in the name of the Lord Jesus. For the promise is for us, for you and for all those whom God has called in his mercy".*

Paul and his companions thus toured several towns and cities, preaching first in synagogues and in public places. They were also invited into homes, and taught believers all about the Kingdom of God. Alexander, given his African experience, was responsible for organizing the groups, while Rufus trained the leaders. Without realizing it, they were totally absorbed in their work.

After several weeks in the Peninsula, and after having visited many localities, Paul felt that his mission should continue further. He gathered the elders of the churches together and told them that he had to go, but that he left Alexander to take care of them and continue to announce the Good News of the Kingdom throughout Spain. As for Rufus, he will accompany him for the rest of their mission. *"God is great and mighty,"* he declared. *"I am amazed by his grace".*

"Many people have come to the Lord, and great miracles have been done by our hands. Alexandre, I must continue my journey, but I cannot leave all these people to their fate. I entrust them to you. Continue to count on the grace of God and proclaim the Good News throughout the region. Surround yourself with elders who are faithful and quick to teach, and do your work conscientiously. God will never forsake you".

"In fact," Alexander replied, *"the word is spreading faster than I expected. Already in Lecuza, but also in Ecija and in all the cities, there are people*

who receive the Good News and who work zealously for the Gospel. May the Lord help us".

After fasting and praying, they all knelt down and called on the Lord. Paul raised his hands and said, *"Lord, I entrust all these brothers and your work to your grace."*

TIMOTHY

Ephesus was one of the oldest and most important Greek cities in Asia Minor. Located not far from the sea, its port was very dynamic. Rome has made it the capital of its province of Asia. It was also an important cultural center with an important infrastructure. The Ephesians were also very religious, having built a temple for Diana and worshiped her in a significant way. Paul was the first to proclaim the gospel there, followed shortly after by Apollos, a native of Alexandria, an eloquent man who was versed in the Scriptures. Paul resided there for three years, proclaiming the gospel and teaching people who came from all over the area. The number of believers had grown so large that he left Timothy there to take care of them. And this was where John-Mark landed when he arrived in the city.

"I see that the grace of God visited Ephesus. There are a lot of great things happening there," he told Timothy.

"Indeed, the harvest is great, but there are not enough workers," complained the latter. *"And I'm still young, and I'm somewhat lacking in experience. Some people don't take me seriously considering my age,"* he continued.

"Don't pay attention to the critics," replied John-Mark. *"Some people will always find fault with it. Be diligent in doing your work with all your heart, and let the Lord do His. I'll give you a hand, and then, like I told Paul, I'm planning on going to Colossi maybe. But I don't know when yet. I wouldn't be far, as you can see".*

"Thank you Mark," replied Timothy. *"Here the brethren are zealous for the gospel. However, there are many people who try to distract the church from its calling. The worshipers of Diana, the Nicolaitans, and many others. The teaching is therefore very important, and I am in the process of forming people who in turn can pass on the teaching of the apostles. There are also a lot of widows and you need good will to be able to take care of them. Ephesus is a large city and it shines throughout the province of Asia. What we are doing here is having an impact on churches across the region".* Then he added, *"You know, the Ephesians are of a great culture and can be very spiritual. The city is rich and cosmopolitan. The temptation is great, and some let themselves be carried away by the pleasures of the world, and easily let themselves be diverted from the simplicity of the Gospel. The fight is quite different from provincial towns where the people are simpler and less sophisticated. Here, we are observed and scrutinized from all sides. We listen to what people say and we evaluate and we judge. Some have been exposed for their lies and people who call themselves apostles have been exposed. The believers here are courageous and are not afraid to suffer. But eventually they cool down, and you feel like they're doing things out of habit or compulsion, rather than desire and love."*

CATALONIA

*I*n Catalonia, Paul and Rufus arrived in Tortosa. As usual, they went to a synagogue on the first Sabbath after their arrival. They attended the worship service before the rabbi invited Paul to speak. The latter spoke in Greek, and Rufus translated it into Latin because in the audience there were Jews and God-fearers who did not understand Hebrew. *"Grace to you and peace from God our Father and the Lord Jesus Christ. It is precisely this Jesus, the cornerstone that the builders have rejected, but of which God made the main one, that of the corner, that we have come to talk to you …"*

As they left the synagogue, a crowd gathered around them. For the people had learned what had happened in Spain, and how, by the hand of the apostle, miracles and wonders had taken place. They brought in the sick, the paralytics, the blind … Paul and Rufus prayed for them, laid their hands on them, and the people were delivered and healed. Several people asked for baptism.

"Let's go to the nearby Ebro river," Rufus suggested.

"I invite all those who wish to be baptized to join us".

Seeing the crowd following them Paul said to Rufus, *"You see Rufus, there is a lot of work to do here. And already, there are people you can count on. Hurry to teach them, then help them install elders in every church, in cities and villages. I am going back to Rome, entrusting you to the grace of God"*.

THREAT

*I*n Carthage, the atmosphere had grown heavy. People from who knows where, stirred up trouble among the population accusing Christians of all kinds of crimes. They challenged their faith and lashed out at them, even physically at times.

Before the arrival of the Romans, Carthage practiced human sacrifices. The richest families, to guarantee their protection and prosperity, offered their eldest son as a sacrifice to the deities, in particular, Tanit. Roman Venus and Greek Aphrodite. Christians rather compared them to the Astarte of the Scriptures.

But the Romans strictly prohibited this practice which ended up disappearing from official ceremonies. The cult of Tanit has however been maintained in different places, becoming more discreet, even secret. The very name of the land, Mauretania, means in the Libyan language *"the land of Tanit"*.

The arrival of the Gospel in North Africa not only raised awareness of the horror of this practice and its abomination in the eyes of the

Creator, but also made people repent of it, abandoning the worship of that divinity and turning to the one true God.

But some pagan priests did not take a positive view of the desertion of their temples by the population. People took fewer and fewer offerings, and the clergy of these cults became poorer. Despite threats and intimidation, the number of conversions to the worship of God increased. So these priests use all kinds of ploys to get their followers back, including using official authorities.

"There are manipulators who operate in the shadows and who try to convince the governor that our faith is dangerous for the Empire, since we refuse to sacrifice to the Emperor," warned Epnaetus.

"Yes," Alexander replied. *"We should be prepared to defend ourselves before the authorities if they were to ask us to justify ourselves in relation to our faith. We should quickly prepare the brothers and above all, warn them not to respond to provocations"*.

PERSECUTION

*I*n Rome, a violent persecution befell the believers. The capital of the empire was ravaged by a huge fire that destroyed half the city. The quality of the buildings occupied by the working class and the peasants, the insanitary conditions and the bad living conditions facilitated the spread of laziness which carried away the houses built of wood. The devastation caused to the city had stirred the population, and people expressed its anger against the authorities. In addition, there was a rumor that Nero himself had caused the fire to be able to reclaim the land and expand his palace.

Fearing a popular revolt against his rule, the emperor sought out culprits to feed the people. And his gaze turned to the new converts who, anyway, did not recognize him as a divine status. Then, a wave of arrests was orchestrated, and many Christians and Jews were arrested, imprisoned and then executed. Among them was Paul, who had returned to Rome and was thrown into the dungeon under painful conditions. While awaiting his trial, he received a visit from Luke, a Greek doctor whom the authorities did not consider to be a Christian.

"Take your quill Luc. I want to dictate a letter to you for Timothy. I know he still needs counseling. I want to give him some recommendations. I had already sent him one, and I think this will be the last. Don't forget to tell him that I'm in chains again. All have abandoned me, except you, Luc. Tell him to hurry up and join us, remember to bring me my coat. It's so cold in here. May he not forget my books and above all, my scrolls. And that he bring Mark with him. He is useful to me for the ministry."

SOLITUDE

That year, Mark felt very lonely. All his old friends and companions were gone. Peter, James, Barnabas, Paul,... as well as his mother Mary. The other apostles also disappeared. Some have been martyred, and there was no news of other parties spreading the gospel to the four corners of the world, as Jesus instructed. His own childhood friends, Alexander and Rufus, sons of Simon of Cyrene, traveled to the ends of the earth and had no news from them. The Lord's witnesses had gone to join him. Did this mean that the end of the world was near?

In Judea, the war was raging. The Zealot revolt provoked a violent reaction from the Vespasians, who for three years had sent large troops to end the uprising and restore the rule of the Empire. Judea has been put down, and Jerusalem razed to the ground. Of the Temple, there was no stone left on stone, as Jesus had announced a few decades earlier. The Jews were either driven out of the Land of Israel to disperse among the other nations, as Moses prophesied one thousand and five hundred years earlier, or taken captive. Even the fortress of Masada which was the pride of the Jewish resistance was taken by the Roman army. It was said that all the Jews there would have committed suicide so as not to be caught by the Romans.

What should it be done now? Once all were indeed gone, what would be left for the new generations? Would the gospel message suffer as a result? Who can attest to the veracity of the teachings they have received?

An idea was starting to germinate in John-Mark's mind. But the thing he wanted most right now was a homecoming. He needed to withdraw a bit, take shelter and think. Because, aware that he still had a role to play, he needed to be given direction, at least to be inspired, to make the right decisions for the rest of what he still had to do. The safest thing for him was to go back to Cyrene. Where it all started.

Mark was a descendant of the tribe of Levi, as was his cousin Joseph called Barnabas. The Jews had dispersed after the destruction of Solomon's temple by the Babylonians, and many found themselves in the diaspora all around the Mediterranean. Others were deported by the Greeks and Romans, far from Judah and Israel. This was the case for the families of Mark and Barnabas. But they still carried with them the desire to serve God and their people. That's why, wherever they go, they know how to make themselves useful.

Now Mark of Cyrene found himself alone, without Barnabas to encourage him, Peter to support him, or Paul to lead him on new adventures. For the first time, he was alone with his responsibilities and he had to make decisions and assume them. By nearly seventy, he had become completely self-sufficient, and he knew that he didn't have much left to live on.

STOPOVER

*I*n the synagogue of the city of Cyrene, no one knew John-Mark. Hardly a few elders had heard of him, but none of them had ever met him. The rabbi was surprised to learn that this Saturday's visitor was from the region. So he invited him to speak after reading the Law and the Prophets.

"I was born in Cyrene, from a family of priests. I quickly learned to read and write following the teachings of this same synagogue. Alexander and Rufus, the sons of Simon, were my neighbors, and with others we played together in the fields among the sheep and the goats. A few years later, my parents moved to Galilee before settling in Jerusalem. Like all Jews, we awaited the coming of the Messiah, the one who would free us from the yoke of the enemy. It was in Galilee that I knew the Lord when I was still young. From the start, I saw his power through the miracles he performed before our eyes. Then I was very sensitive to his teachings. I had the grace to be one of those who first received the Spirit of God. And since then, I have not stopped traveling the world, to participate in the proclamation of the glory of God, alongside Barnabas, Simon Peter and Paul. I accompanied Barnabas and Paul to Antioch and Cyprus, then traveled with Simon Peter

to Asia and Babylon. I went to Colossi, Ephesus and Italy. I have known the Lord's Apostles and many other servants of God.

The work is growing, and I am glad to see that here and elsewhere, lives are transformed, and many have turned from evil to walk in the ways of righteousness.

Something in my heart tells me that my journey does not end here in Cyrene, although I am happy to have returned to my hometown and my roots. I am going to stay with you for a while, and then I will have to resume my journey. But hoping to see you again soon. I ask you to pray for me, for I will continue my calling".

ALEXANDRIA

It was hot in Alexandria. John-Mark had just arrived, and he had decided to visit the city. He was already impressed, like all travelers visiting the city, by the grandeur of the lighthouse built at the end of the port, but on top of that, it almost felt like Greece. In the city, there were many temples dedicated to several deities, a large Forum, thermal baths like the Romans, and also a large amphitheater, witnesses of a wealth of leisure activities. The rich and commercial city served as a link between Upper Egypt and the rest of the world. Goods poured in by the river and the economic dynamism caused the noise to be incessant. Alexandria was bigger and more important than Cyrene, and you met people from all over the place.

The goal of John-Mark was, as usual, to go to the synagogue on the Sabbath day. He was planning on renting a house to settle in while he waited to see how things would turn out for him.

As he walked through the city under the hot Egyptian sun, his sandal tore. He dragged it as best as he could, in the direction of the forum where there were many stalls. Stores of all kinds sold both local and imported products: fruits and vegetables, spices, clothing, fabrics, pottery, jewelry, etc. Others offered repair services for objects of all kinds. There are also blacksmiths, carpenters, tailors and shoemakers.

"*Sit down,*" said the shoemaker to whom John-Mark showed his sandal. "*I'll take care of you right away. Aren't you from here?*"

"*I'm from Cyrene,*" Mark replied. "*I don't know your city well. It is beautiful, but so tall*".

"*Let's see this sandal. It has suffered a lot, it seems. Do you walk a lot? Your accent tells me that you come from further than Cyrene*".

"*It's true, I come from a lot of places at the same time. From Jerusalem, Antioch, Rome … wherever the Lord leads me*".

While the two men chatted, the shoemaker took a long needle, threaded thick thread through the cat, and began his work.

"*Today I am in Alexandria, and tomorrow who knows where I might be? And it's true that I like to walk. As much as it depends on me, I move more easily when I do not depend on donkeys, camels or horses*", John-Mark added.

Suddenly, the shoemaker cried out: "*One God!* "The long needle had just pierced his hand. Blood gushed out, and flowed profusely. The shoemaker withdrew the needle from his aching hand, but the blood continued to flow. He looked for a compress to press on his wound and stop the blood. But it continued to flow.

So Mark said to him: "*let me do*". He spat on the ground and made a ball of mud, then said, "*Give me your hand.*"

Mark applied the ball of mud to the shoemaker's hand, and the blood immediately stopped flowing, and the wound closed.

"Rinse your hand now. You are healed".

The shoemaker did so and found that the wound had completely closed and there was not even a scar left. He exclaimed, *"One God, great and mighty! "*Then, looking at Mark, he asked in astonishment: *"But who are you?"*

"I am a servant of this Unique God whom you invoke without knowing him", answered Mark. *"He created the heavens and the earth and everything in it. He sent his only son to save us from the evil that gnaws at us and to make us his children".*

"My name is Anianus," said the shoemaker. *"Please allow me the honor to come to my house and tell us about this God who sent you to us".*

HUNT

*I*n Carthage, the persecution was severe. The hunt for Christians had started and arrests were being made among them. The trials were expeditious, and several believers were executed.

Epnaetus, speaking to the community, reported on the situation and provided his recommendations. *"The persecution is fierce. Take care of yourself, your families and the brothers. Do not expose yourself unnecessarily, but strengthen all believers. Let those who can go elsewhere, to other towns and cities, while awaiting the end of these persecutions, do so. Others, do not stop praying. Do not return evil for evil, and do not respond to any provocation. But be ready to give an account for your faith. May this serve as a testimony to our executioners. Most importantly, don't forget to pray for those who persecute you. Alexander, Photina, and many other brothers and sisters paid with their lives for not denying their faith. They are very happy now with the Lord. May the grace of God be upon you all".*

After Rome, it was Carthage's turn to experience persecution. The authorities imagined they could intimidate Christians and thus stifle this new faith which was so different from pagan cults. But the more they persecuted believers, the more conversions there were.

Even around the governor and in the military. The conversions also affected merchants, peasants, teachers,… What infuriated pagan religious leaders was that even among them, several priests believed and were baptized, abandoning idolatrous and witchcraft practices.

The governor knew very well that he could do nothing against this movement which was out of control. But he could not stand idly by, lest, on hearing this, Rome would get angry with him and remove him from office. So he redoubled his zeal, multiplied the trials and made the sentences more and more severe.

THUNDERSTORMS

*I*n Catalonia, the atmosphere was totally different from that in Carthage. The preaching of the gospel attracted more and more people, and the transformation of lives called for the adoption of this new faith. What most affected Jewish believers was that the proclamation of Jesus Christ in no way contradicted the faith of Abraham professed by Moses, but completed it perfectly. It was obvious that this Jesus was indeed the long awaited Messiah. Because the synagogues were regularly crossed by various religious currents which sowed the disorder among the believers. From time to time, people appeared who claimed to be the Messiah and diverted believers from the true worship of God. Since then, the rabbis and the elders have taken care that nothing disturbs the tranquility of the synagogues. What was different that time was that the preachers, whether they were Paul or Rufus, did not contradict the Scriptures in any way, but instead relied on and confirmed them. Moreover, the transformed lives, the performed miracles testified in favor of this new faith which made so much good.

The new believers would spontaneously proclaim the Good News everywhere on their way. Christian communities were spontaneously formed, and Rufus could not help but note the zeal of the Catalans for the word of God. They were thirsty without knowing it, and now that they found it, they not only drank from it, but also shared it with everyone else thirsty in their communities. Tortosa served only as a base. The number of conversions taking place everywhere else was impossible to assess. And the feedback that Simon of Cyrene's son was receiving clearly reminded him of what his brother Alexander had told him about North Africa.

Rufus addressing a group of disciples: *"Brothers from Valencia, having heard the Word of God here in Tortosa, ask us to go to their homes to proclaim the Gospel there and to teach them more about things that concern the Lord Jesus. I'll go there with some brothers. Then I have resolved to cross the Pyrenees to announce the grace of God in the Narbonese Gaul. By His grace, I will continue my journey where the Lord guides me, after I establish a church and help install elders".*

MANUSCRIPT

In Alexandria, The Shoemaker was happy to receive Mark at home. He brought together all of his people, as well as a few neighbors, having invited them to listen to the Cyrenean speak of the invisible God whom they invoke without knowing him.

Mark taught Anianus and his entourage to speak, and every day more and more people followed the teachings.

"Your house is gathering a real church of God now. We should train people capable of transmitting this teaching throughout Egypt, in order to benefit as many people as possible. For the Kingdom of God is great, and it is open to whoever wants to enter it, for the sacrifice of Jesus washes the sins of whoever calls on the name of the Lord".

"You know Mark," said Anianus, *"the tradition with us since the days of the pharaohs has been to write down important things on papyri. It would be nice if people could take something with them so that they could share it with others. If you could write down what you teach us, we can make copies and send them all over Egypt".*

"It's a great idea Anianus," Mark replied. *"This was exactly the direction I expected from God. He just spoke through your mouth. I will write a manuscript in which I will tell the gospel of Jesus Christ, the son of God. For now, I have planned to visit Deep Egypt, and on my return, I will take the time to do so. But in the meantime, if there are people with good memories, encourage them to share this wherever they go. The scrolls of the Law and the Prophets already contain all the teachings that I have given you".*

"Let me come with you on your tour. I know the country well, and I will be useful to you on this trip".

GAUL

*A*fter crossing the Pyrenees, Rufus let himself be led to his new destination, while announcing the Good News of the Kingdom on his way. In Narbone, the enthusiasm of the people for the gospel astonished those who accompanied the son of Simon of Cyrene. *"The harvest is great for those who are willing to take the trouble to work,"* said Rufus. *"Everywhere we go people are looking for the truth, and their souls need deliverance and rest. It is enough to present to them the one whose burden is light and the yoke easy. Let us work, as Paul said, and do not slack off. We can rest later, when we are with the Lord"*.

Rufus continued to advance eastward, crossing southern Gaul, alongside the sea. For this is where there are ports and the trading posts attracted a lot of people. In addition, there are many fishing villages. *"You fish for fish, but if you follow the Lord, you will be like me, fishers of men,"* he said. *"The Kingdom of God is so vast that we can enjoy it into Eternity. The older I get, the more I rejoice in the Eternal life that the Lord has given me"*.

Arriving in Avignon, Rufus felt that this was the end of his journey and the culmination of his stay on this land. He worked tirelessly, preaching, teaching and discipling. *"I will not delay joining the Lord any longer, but you persevere and continue to announce this Good News of the Kingdom. In your turn, train disciples, people able to go to the most remote regions to transmit the message of God's love for all men. In this city of Avignon, a house should be built to serve the work of the Lord".*

Having traveled the region, little by little Rufus finally found the place that seemed best suited for his project.

"We will build on this rock a place that can receive people, and which will serve as a base for the proclamation of the gospel throughout the region. I thank God for the welcome we received in this city and the many people who responded to his call".

GOSPEL

After having isolated himself for several days in Cyrene, Mark returned to find the growing number of brothers, a manuscript in his arms.

"I was worried that the brothers would disperse or be drawn into unnecessary arguments. So I decided to use all the resources available to me, and my own experience since meeting the Lord Jesus in Galilee when I was still young. I also used many testimonies from Simon Peter who was a Father to me, from my cousin Barnabas who always encouraged me, and from Paul with whom I worked a lot. I have written a book to tell what the Lord has done and taught, and which is the gospel of Jesus Christ, Son of God, to leave a mark on future generations. I made sure it wasn't too long so that it could be read in assemblies, portion by portion, to give the brethren a chance to memorize it.

Here in Cyrene there are many copyists. I would like copies of this gospel to be sent to Jerusalem, Cyprus, Antioch and Alexandria. I myself would send copies to the brothers in Carthage and Rome. After that, I plan to go back to Alexandria. There is still work to be done there".

Cyrene was a prosperous city. The intermingling of populations of different origins stimulated the region and made it possible to retain what was best in them. In addition, its geographical location was favorable to trade. There were endless journeys between Cyrene, Alexandria and Crete. Cyrene has seen the birth of many philosophers, rhetoricians, mathematicians, geographers, grammarians and all kinds of scholars in various specialties having published numerous treatises and works circulating throughout the Empire. Athens and Alexandria had benefited particularly well, alongside Rome, Ephesus, Corinth and Antioch. Without counting Jerusalem and Carthage. The studious atmosphere of the Pentapolis was therefore favorable to the publication of a book recounting the facts and teachings of Jesus of Nazareth.

MARTYR

*I*n Alexandria, some people were furious at the success of the preaching of the gospel. More and more pagans were turning away from idols and the temples were visibly emptying. The pagan priests complained about the drop in offerings, and tried to frighten their devotees by threatening them with the wrath of the gods. But nothing helped, the Christians were more and more numerous, and this desertion of the pagan temples was attributed to the stranger who came from Cyrene, John-Mark.

A large crowd surrounded the Christians who accompanied Mark to the place of the forum, cursing them, insulting them and threatening them with all kinds of reprisals.

From among the crowd, a man who appeared to be a priest of Amun, made accusations: *"These people are diverting the people from worshiping our gods. And since this Mark arrived in Alexandria, our temples are emptying, while their basilicas keep filling up. He harms our gods and the emperor. Let's stop him, tie him by the neck, and drag him through the streets of the city to teach him not to prey on our gods anymore"*.

The crowd was excited. They surrounded Mark and some men put the rope around his neck. At the end of this rope, he was tied to an ox which dragged him, pushed by the howls of the delirious crowd, in the streets of the city. Mark fell, but the ox didn't stop. He was going faster and faster, dragging Mark to the ground.

When he arrived at the fishing port, he was tied up, while his body was bloodied. The priest, raising his voice to be heard by the crowd said: *"Let's throw him in jail. It's getting late. We will come back tomorrow to take care of him"*.

Inside the cold and unsanitary prison, Mark found a place to lie down. His body was bruised and the pains were hardly bearable. Blood from his head covered his face, and his torn clothes hinted at the wounds on his elbows and knees. His neck was severely irritated from the friction of the rope that had been put on him during the day. His feet bled so much that he had difficulty standing. But he still had the strength to pray.

"Father, here my race ends. I have spoken your word and obeyed your commandments. I have fought the good fight of faith and I rejoice that you have found me worthy to suffer for you. It is not for myself that I pray, but for all those who have received your word in this city and wherever I have announced it. Cause the word that comes out of their mouth to bear fruit even into eternal life. I also pray for my tormentors. I ask you not to impute this sin to them, and to extend your grace in their favor, so that their hearts may be illuminated and that they may recognize that you alone are God".

Early in the morning, after a cold and humid night, Mark is awakened by the sound of a crowd which, again, gathered in front of the prison gates.

"Thank you Lord, and may my brothers not have to suffer from my martyrdom."

A guard opened the prison door, and someone put a rope around Mark's neck again, then dragged him outside, to the shrill cries of the crowd. Then Mark is dragged through the streets once again.

After long minutes of collective hysteria, a voice was heard shouting: *"He's dead, he's dead!"*

But the crowd shouted louder and louder, *"Long live our gods, and glory to the Emperor!"*

So someone suggested throwing Mark's body on the rocks and burning it.

In anger, two men lifted the body and dragged it to the seashore, throwing it onto a rock. They covered it with wood and oil, and set it on fire. The hysterical crowd cried again louder and louder.

Suddenly the sky darkened, and a downpour of rain fell so hard that it extinguished the burning fire to burn the martyr. Sudden panic took hold of the crowd, which began to run in all directions. In no time, the place was deserted. As soon as the rain stopped, some disciples who were watching the scene from afar approached and retrieved the body to bury it further.

Mark's body was embalmed in a chapel near the port. Someone closed the door and said:

"Now Lord, let the testimony of your servants be spread over the whole earth, and let your word be proclaimed to every man as you have commanded us."

AVIGNON

*I*n Avignon, the chapel desired by Rufus was erected on the rock chosen by him. Many people came to visit and receive the teachings necessary to grow in faith. Many could not read or write, but Rufus enjoyed reading to them the text of the gospel written by his brother and childhood friend, John-Mark, despite his advanced age and his weaker eyes. Rufus knew how to tell the stories he had lived or heard about, captivating his audience of many young and old. Every verse, every passage of Mark's gospel reminded him of something. Reading what his friend had reported, Rufus relived the events and felt himself rejuvenated. He was so happy to know that a written record of Jesus' life finally existed. And even more, when he learned that other witnesses had also written documents: Matthew and John, while Luke took the time to collect the testimony of those who personally knew the Lord to tell his story.

John, the disciple whom Jesus loved was arrested and then reportedly thrown alive into a pot of boiling oil. But John escaped unscathed, much like Daniel and his companions escaped the blazing furnace unscathed.

Tired of the old man's resistance, the Romans decided to keep him away from the Christians by isolating him on the island of Patmos. Upon hearing the news, Rufus made a remark that made his audience smile: *"When are the Romans going to realize that one cannot fight against the living God?"*

Some time later, the younger son of Simon of Cyrene went to join the Lord. One of the elders spoke in the new chapel and said: *"Rufus, son of Simon of Cyrene and brother of our beloved Alexander, recommended that we follow Jesus' command. Each carry their cross and go all over the world to announce the Good News. From here we will go everywhere, as the other brothers do, and we pray that no one will be deprived of the grace of God"*.